The Agile Manager's Guide To

COACHING TO
MAXIMIZE PERFORMANCE

The Agile Manager's Guide To

COACHING TO
MAXIMIZE PERFORMANCE

By Jack Cullen and Len D'Innocenzo

Velocity Business Publishing
Bristol, Vermont USA

For Grace and Jack Cullen and Nina and Frank D'Innocenzo
With love and grateful appreciation for
your guidance and inspiration

Copyright © 1999 by D'Innocenzo-Cullen & Associates, LLC

All Rights Reserved

Printed in the United States of America

Library of Congress Catalog Card Number 99-64995

ISBN 1-58099-016-9

Title page illustration by Elayne Sears

The information on behavioral styles is adapted from the widely used DiSC® Model and the Personal Profile System®. The Personal Profile System is copyrighted (©) 1994 by Carlson Learning Company, Minneapolis, Minnesota. DiSC® and Personal Profile System® are registered trademarks of Carlson Learning Company. Used with permission.

If you'd like additional copies of this book or a catalog of books in the Agile Manager Series™, please get in touch.

- **Write us:**
  Velocity Business Publishing, Inc.
  15 Main Street
  Bristol, VT 05443 USA

- **Call or fax us:**
  1-888-805-8600 in North America (toll-free)
  1-802-453-6669 from all other countries
  1-802-453-2164 (fax)

- **E-mail us:**
  action@agilemanager.com

- **Visit our Web site:**
  www.agilemanager.com

To get in touch with Jack Cullen or Len D'Innocenzo, call 1-609-730-0395, 1-978-474-8657, or visit their Web site, www.dcandassoc.com.

Contents

Books in the Agile Manager Series™:

Giving Great Presentations
Understanding Financial Statements
Motivating People
Making Effective Decisions
Leadership
Goal-Setting and Achievement
Delegating Work
Cutting Costs
Influencing People
Effective Performance Appraisals
Writing to Get Action
Hiring Excellence
Building and Leading Teams
Getting Organized
Extraordinary Customer Service
Customer-Focused Selling
Managing Irritating People
Coaching to Maximize Performance

Chapter One

Coach Your Way To Success

"Do what you say you'll do!"

THE GOLDEN RULE OF COACHING

Things were not going well for the Agile Manager's new sales team. Five months ago, he was asked to take over the largest sales district in the region. The previous district manager had become complacent, and sales were off two years in a row. A change needed to be made, and the Agile Manager was thought to be the right person to get the district back on track.

The first quarter of the new fiscal year had just ended and sales in the district were half of what they should have been. The salespeople weren't happy about their performance, and neither was the Agile Manager. The salespeople blamed the lack of sales on an important new product line that was not available for delivery during the quarter. They said they couldn't sell enough of the older product lines to make their quota.

Morale was low because sales and commissions were low, and people were asking the Agile Manager to lower their quotas because the new product line was delayed.

This was not a good situation.

Making matters worse, in the eyes of the sales force, the new product line was not going to be available for delivery until late in the second quarter. The Agile Manager felt the delay might even stretch into the third quarter and put the entire year's business plan in jeopardy.

But the sales team needed to focus their efforts on what they could do, and not worry about the things that were out of their control. The Agile Manager had been delivering this message to the team since taking over. And while everyone said they understood, no one was really listening.

He decided to take action. He needed to capture the attention of the team and coach them on how to be successful in this situation. And he had just the thing: Bring in a successful salesperson from another district.

The Agile Manager knew how important it was to employ different coaching styles. He didn't always need to be the person telling the team how to do something. He knew that a good method for coaching a team is to ask a successful person to talk about what he or she did to succeed, and how to avoid mistakes. Even the skeptics on a team will listen intently to one of their peers who is succeeding when they are having problems.

The successful salesman he had in mind, Charlie Adams, had over twenty years of experience and was able to meet his quota during the last quarter by selling what was available. When he asked Charlie to help him coach the other people on how to make their numbers even though the new product line was delayed, Charlie said he was happy to help.

Charlie lit up a room when he walked in. He was tall with a head of snow-white hair, loud, and always smiling. Charlie was also familiar with new product delays. He'd seen plenty of them during his career. And the first time it happened, he fell behind in his quota—just as the Agile Manager's people had—waiting for a new product release.

But Charlie learned from both his successes and failures. He tried never to make the same mistake twice. Regarding new product releases, Charlie's policy was, "Sell the solutions that are available today. Don't propose the new ones until they are ready for delivery." This policy helped Charlie exceed his quota year in and year out.

To better capture the attention of the team, he asked Charlie if he would mind sharing his income figure from the previous year with the sales team. Charlie was proud of the fact that he was one of the top producers in the company year after year, and so he agreed.

To illustrate this point, and to enhance Charlie's credibility, the Agile Manager made a huge poster-size copy of Charlie's W-2 earnings report from the previous year. This poster would be unveiled at the meeting and remain in sight during Charlie's presentation. The point: If Charlie could earn a substantial income in the current sales environment by following the fundamentals, so could the other people on the team.

Charlie's W-2 was exactly the attention grabber that the Agile Manager wanted. From the moment it was uncovered, most people could not stop staring at it. It was twice what any other salesperson in the room had earned the previous year. If Charlie had a secret that would help them to succeed, they wanted to know. They listened to Charlie talk about how executing the fundamentals each day can lead to financial success. A great coaching session was under way, and the Agile Manager enjoyed it all from the back of the room.

Good coaches can develop the untapped potential of their people and improve results considerably. That's why smart business leaders today empower managers to coach and develop their people.

Our company, D'Innocenzo-Cullen & Associates, helps growth-oriented companies improve results through leadership and coaching workshops. We also help set up systems that develop individual skills and improve performance. In this book, we'll share our expertise with you.

Don't Just Manage—Coach!

Let's get one thing straight from the outset: There's a big difference between managing and coaching. Managing has to do with the process of business. Managers control tangible assets like plant and equipment, or inventory and accounts receivable.

Managers also control their time, long-term business plans, and budgets. Managers watch over assets, implement policy, follow prescribed procedures, and enforce company policy.

All these things are important, of course. But the best managers are also good coaches. They care about people, ideas, innovation, and imagination. They inspire and empower their people to create reality from dreams. They lead by example and serve as role models for the entire organization.

Best Tip

Don't be afraid to make mistakes—all good leaders do. As you master your defeats, you'll become a better coach.

Good managers who know how to coach their people make excellent leaders. The best leader/coaches have a vision for their people. They influence them to do things that are important and necessary. They intentionally create the right motivational environment. They are interested in their people as human beings, and in helping them develop to their full potential. They coach and counsel their people and, when necessary, confront them in a caring and constructive way.

It's the leadership qualities of the top business coaches that inspire people to work to achieve spectacular heights and overcome extraordinary problems.

Can Anyone Coach?

Many people today are caught up in a "management mystique" that suggests that good managers experience one success after another. This idea is simply incorrect. Top-flight business managers make plenty of mistakes along the way.

You don't need to be perfect to be a coach. Good business coaches grow from mastering their defeats. They know that life is rarely a steady progression of successes—one consecutive "win" after another. The important thing, any coach can tell you, is to learn from your mistakes and defeats.

You also don't have to be a certain kind of person to be a

good coach. You can be successful no matter what your personality. The only requirements are that you care about your people and that you want to improve the area you manage.

YOUR JOB AS COACH

You have six important jobs to do as coach. Let's go over them one by one.

1. Establish Your Credibility

You'll build credibility and earn loyalty by proving—again and again—that you're honest, trustworthy, competent, and respectful of each individual. Demonstrating dedication to your people and to your mission also builds credibility and helps you through the most difficult times.

Your credibility as a coach is usually earned slowly and can be lost quickly. Your people will consider you to be a credible coach when you demonstrate the following:

Honesty
- They know where you stand
- They know where they stand
- You are consistent in your actions
- You follow through on commitments
- You stand up for your beliefs

Competence
- You know the business well
- You lead by example
- You develop strategic and tactical plans
- You can solve problems

Inspiration
- You have good people skills
- You are enthusiastic
- You communicate well
- You like to have fun
- You know what your people want and help them get it

- You build consensus by asking for input

Vision
- You provide clear goals and direction
- You have a forward-looking mission
- You know the company's goals
- You communicate the "Big Picture"

The importance of credibility for a business coach cannot be overstated. Good coaches must be credible if they want to influence and develop their people.

Why? People rarely make a decision to listen or follow someone unless that person establishes credibility and trust with them. When people make decisions that affect their jobs and their lives, the personal side—"who am I dealing with?"—always enters the picture.

The fact is, for people to accept you as their coach, they must believe you're credible. When you establish credibility, you have a better opportunity to help them develop so they can accomplish great things. Without establishing credibility, you may be considered their manager, but you'll never be considered their coach. Take it to the bank!

2. Set and Communicate Goals and Expectations

Goals are the key to success. Good coaches empower their people with the right set of tools to achieve defined goals.

But remember: You can't do a goal. You do activities. That's why good coaches monitor the important activities of their people. When your people are doing the right activities, they will achieve their goals.

Good coaches also clarify their expectations of success for their people. This means both team success and individual success. One without the other indicates a coach's lack of interest in the individual's success, which can produce negative consequences down the road.

Once people know what is expected of them, it is important

for the team to let the coach know what they expect in return. Setting and communicating expectations together greatly reduces the need for confrontations later.

3. Plan for Success

One of the most important activities for a coach to do is to plan. Yet most people don't spend enough time planning. Why? "Not enough time" is one common excuse.

Many managers were promoted because they were successful individual performers—doing things. As a coach, you need to direct the activities of your people, which involves more thinking and analyzing instead of acting and reacting. The best way we know to direct activities successfully is by planning effectively.

> **Best Tip**
>
> Take time to establish your credibility. Without it, people won't accept you as their coach and leader.

You may want to involve your people during a planning session. This helps them to take ownership of the plan and is a great team-building activity.

Bill Walsh, a football strategist and former head coach of the San Francisco 49ers, is worth studying. Walsh prepared for each football game by planning out the first twenty-five plays his offense would run.

Walsh would follow his game plan and run those twenty-five plays. No matter what happened—fumbles, interceptions, or even if his team scored a touchdown—nothing would derail the plan. Walsh's objective was to see how his opponent would react to specific formations.

After the twenty-five plays, he analyzed the defense to determine strengths and weaknesses. Walsh then called plays that took advantage of the other team's weaknesses, while avoiding the strengths. Walsh's 49ers were so successful with this approach that they won the NFL World Championship three times.

Advanced planning by head coaches makes winners on the

football field. Good planning will likewise make you a winning coach in business.

4. Give Feedback on Performance and Facilitate Work

Coaches need to direct the activities of their people to achieve specific results. To get good results, coach and counsel your people.

Best Tip

Lead by example every day. Your credibility as a coach depends upon it.

Also, facilitate work for your new people by taking the time to explain the steps required to do specific tasks. Don't assume they know how to do something, especially if they are new.

A common mistake managers make is to assume their people know how to do things. We suggest you ask. Give people a chance to tell you where they need coaching from you. Encourage them to come to you with specific types of problems. And don't do their work for them—coach them on "how" to do things instead of just telling them "what" to do.

Even with veteran people that may be new to your team, make time early on to be sure they understand what you need them to do. When necessary, explain the way you want things done. Set your expectations and be clear with your directions. Ask them if they understand the process you want them to follow.

You may also want to ask if they have another way to get something done. Experienced performers usually will have "their way" of doing things. Make sure their way will work and follows company policy. If not, suggest another way of doing things.

Then, observe your people in action to see what they do well and where they may need help. We will go into greater detail on the specific hands-on coaching steps you should follow in chapter six.

Provide both positive and constructive feedback, and make recommendations and adjustments that will improve performance. This is the counseling part of your job. Different people will have different needs. Depending on their level of development, you'll need to make different recommendations. We cover this in greater detail in chapter five. Understand, too, that people want their positive actions and accomplishments recognized publicly. They will also prefer to have any negative actions discussed privately to preserve their egos. Be sensitive to your people's needs and always avoid embarrassing them.

5. Lead by Example

Good coaches lead by example every day. Good leader/coaches never ask their people to do things they would not do.

Good coaches nonetheless need to be willing to delegate certain activities to subordinates. This is one of the best ways to help people develop their skills. It helps prepare people for greater responsibility. It also allows you to focus more of your time on coaching and developing people, rather than doing tasks.

Good coaches also know how to manage time. They convey a sense of urgency to their people regarding activities, large or small. They take an interest in their people's well being and model the good behaviors and activities they want employees to follow.

6. Motivate, Build Morale, and Attend to Interpersonal Relations

While motivation comes from within each person, creating a motivational environment is the responsibility of every coach. People will work hard to achieve specific goals if their manager/coach can spark their motivational drives.

In professional sports, for example, the talent level of the athletes is usually similar. Good coaches are highly paid when they motivate their teams to do extraordinary things.

To help your team be successful, you need to watch them in action. Get to know what each person on your team does best and where each could improve. Support their positive actions and efforts, guide their direction and, when appropriate, instruct or demonstrate more effective techniques.

Keep an open-door policy, too. It helps build morale. So does showing an interest in the development of your subordinates and providing them with opportunities for growth. Finding reasons to like each of your people creates a strong team atmosphere and reduces tension.

The Agile Manager's Checklist

✔ Work at being a good coach. You can improve results considerably.

✔ Remember that credibility is your most important asset as a coach.

✔ Demonstrate, on a daily basis, honesty, competence, inspiration, and vision.

✔ Empower your people with the right set of tools to achieve well-defined goals.

✔ Plan ahead. That's what makes winning coaches—in either sports or business.

Chapter Two

Coach According to Style

"Whether it's sports or business, winning and losing doesn't depend on trick plays or new systems. It comes down to motivating people to work hard and prepare to play as a team that really counts. In a word, it's Coaching!"

Don Shula

We have encountered many successful coaches. Some were strict disciplinarians who expected much of their people and who were direct when giving instruction. Some used a more relaxed, softer, lower-key style. Some were enthusiastic and often emotional. And others were sticklers for detail who followed prescribed manners to the letter.

These "types" reflect the four major coaching styles, and all are effective. You can be even more effective, however, if you can adapt your style to the person you're coaching. That's because the best style to use depends on the individual and the situation. The best coaches have the skill (versatility) and the will (flexibility) to change their coaching style as the people and situation change.

In its DiSC® System, Carlson Learning Company, of Minneapolis, Minnesota, identifies the major personality or behavior styles. We've used the DiSC® system in our work for years with great success.*

While some people blend styles, you'll probably see yourself most strongly in one or two of them. Knowing your style can give you insight into your personality and help you coach better.

The styles also describe, of course, the people you coach. Each person will have unique characteristics that require you to adapt your approach.

Let's review each of the four styles. Then, in the next chapter, we'll show you how to create the right motivational environment for different people depending on their personality styles.

The Dominance Style (High D)

The easiest personality to recognize is the Dominance Style. Dominance types are direct and forceful. They usually talk fast, have definite opinions, and like to make things happen. They enjoy—even thrive on—challenges.

They strive to shape their environment by overcoming opposition and getting the results they want.

Those with the Dominance Style of personality like to:

- Get immediate results
- Cause action
- Accept challenges
- Make quick decisions
- Take authority
- Manage trouble

Such people like a work environment that gives them opportunities to gain power and authority, prestige, and recognition. They have a strong need to accomplish their goals, and they will overcome (or run over) obstacles.

---

*The ideas that follow are adapted from Carlson Learning Company's DiSC® Model and Personal Profile System®. We strongly endorse both. (DiSC® and Personal Profile System® are registered trademarks of Carlson Learning Company.)

Some public figures who demonstrate High D behavior: former Prime Minister Margaret Thatcher; New York Yankees owner George Steinbrenner; football coaches Mike Ditka, Bill Parcells, and Jimmy Johnson; and basketball coach Bobby Knight. Their motto is usually something like "Just do it!"

The Influence Style (High i)

The second personality style that is easy to recognize is the Influence Style. These people shape the environment by bringing others into alliance to get results. Like the Dominance personality, those of the Influence Style also want results. But they also care about people. They influence others to see things their way and enjoy public recognition for their accomplishments.

This style enjoys dealing with people, making a favorable impression, talking things through, creating a good motivational environment, and viewing people and situations optimistically. They desire an environment that includes popularity, social recognition, public recognition of ability, freedom of expression, and freedom from control and details.

Best Tip

Take time to understand what makes your employees (and you) tick. Doing so will take some of the mystery out of coaching.

They are excellent communicators who always try to make a good first impression. They motivate their people and love to generate enthusiasm. They entertain tirelessly and enjoy helping others.

They will chat with you about anything on their minds. But you may have a problem keeping their interest when you start to chat about the "details."

Some public figures with this style: Presidents Bill Clinton and John F. Kennedy, Muhammad Ali, television talk show host Oprah Winfrey, basketball coach Pat Riley, and football star Deion Sanders. Their motto could be "People make work fun," or "To know me is to love me."

The Steadiness Style (High S)

The Steadiness Style likes to cooperate with others to carry out a task. They are team players and prefer dealing with things, one thing at a time. Count on the High S to complete his or her assignments.

High S's are patient, loyal, and will always listen to somebody else's problems. They want to fit into the group. They have mastered a special skill—they are great at calming down excited people. Steadiness personalities have traditional values and like to receive credit for their work. They don't like changes, especially abrupt changes. They appreciate an orderly step-by-step approach.

This person's tendencies include performing in a consistent, predictable manner; creating a stable, harmonious work environment; demonstrating patience and loyalty; and being a good listener. High S's desire security in any situation, like the status quo unless you supply good reasons to change, hope for your validation of their self-worth, and want guidelines for accomplishing the task.

Best Tip
Adapt your style to the personality type of the person you're coaching. You'll get results much faster.

Some public figures that demonstrate High S behavior: President George Bush, golf great Jack Nicklaus, basketball star Michael Jordan and coach Larry Bird, and baseball "iron man" Cal Ripken, Jr. Their motto could be "Steady the course," or, "If it's not broken, don't fix it."

The Conscientiousness Style (High C)

The Conscientiousness Style is cautious and demands quality. Those with this personality follow standards, preferably *their* standards. They are sticklers for detail, and they want to work under known conditions and written procedures.

The High C type of personality will always follow the rules.

They are critical thinkers and love to check for accuracy. They dislike sudden changes, because they need time to analyze the reasons for the change. They take more time making a decision because they need more information or will need to double-check something.

This person pays attention to key directives and standards, concentrates on the details, thinks analytically, weighs pros and cons, and uses systematic approaches to situations or activities. This person desires a work environment that defines performance expectations, values quality and accuracy, provides opportunities to demonstrate expertise, allows control over factors that affect performance, and offers a reserved, businesslike atmosphere.

Some public figures that come to mind: President Jimmy Carter, Vice President Al Gore, Federal Reserve Board Chairman Alan Greenspan, Jacqueline Kennedy Onassis, Senator Bob Dole, basketball coach Phil Jackson, and hockey great Wayne Gretzky. Their motto might be "Anything worth doing is worth doing right," or, "Quality is job one."

As Charlie Adams continued talking about the fundamentals that helped him to be successful, one participant was skeptical.

Paul, a High D or Dominance Style person with a lot of experience, interrupted Charlie in the middle of his coaching session and said, "That's all well and good Charlie, but our customers are different. When we promise them new products, they expect us to deliver."

Charlie looked directly at Paul and recognized from the tone in his voice that his was a High D style. Charlie responded directly to Paul's interruption.

"What makes you think your customers are any different from mine?" asked Charlie. Without waiting for Paul to respond, Charlie said, "My customers expect delivery as promised, too. I make it a point, Paul, to promise only what I know I can deliver. That's why you need to set the right expectations with your customers from the start."

Paul was caught off guard by Charlie's direct response. Paul also knew Charlie was correct, and he respected his direct approach. "You're right, Charlie. I guess I sometimes promise things that I hope will happen instead of promising what I can make happen. It happened to me this year."

Charlie said, "Paul, it's happened to all of us at some time in our career."

Just then, Jill, a twenty-something junior rep, jumped into the conversation. "I had the same thing happen to me this year, too," said Jill. "One of my best customers was pressing me for information on our new product line. I felt I had to tell him what I knew. I thought I was giving him accurate information. But it was incomplete. Boy, did that backfire on me."

Reading Jill as a High I, or Influencing style, with an eagerness to talk, Charlie said, "Can you tell us how giving incomplete information hurt you with the customer, Jill?"

"Well, I thought explaining some of the new product's features would give us an advantage in the eyes of the customer," said Jill.

"And why didn't it? How did this backfire on you?" asked Charlie.

"They liked what I was saying about the new product line so much, they canceled their orders for the current product line," replied Jill. "They said they'd rather wait for the new product line to arrive. I was afraid they'd cancel altogether and buy from our competition if the new products weren't available in time. So I told them the earliest date the new products would be available. I figured that's the best way to save the account."

"What happened next?" asked Charlie.

"When the new product delivery date started slipping back and back, the customer became more and more impatient. I started off on the wrong foot with a good customer and they ended up not buying anything at all from us," explained Jill

Charlie asked, "What did you learn from that experience?"

"I learned not to discuss new products until they were ready for delivery," responded Jill. "If I had not mentioned anything about them, the customer would have been happy with the older product line. It's working fine for them. I didn't need to explain that much. I was too product-focused and too talkative."

Charlie noticed that one of the other reps, Cliff, was nodding in agreement. He had not spoken at all during the meeting, and Charlie wasn't sure if he was a High S (Steadiness) or High C (Conscientiousness) style. They are similar because they tend to be quiet and reserved.

Charlie said "Cliff, you seem to be in agreement with Jill. Has something similar happened to you this year?"

It seemed to take Cliff a while to respond to Charlie's question. Charlie waited patiently.

After about ten seconds, Cliff replied, "I would never promise a customer something I wasn't sure was going to happen. People want to get information they can rely on. But that was one of my problems last year. I was uncomfortable talking about our new product line at all. I thought it best to wait until the new line was released before I'd discuss it at all. I lost a big deal because of that."

"Would you mind sharing what happened to you, Cliff?" asked Charlie. "I think we could all benefit from your experience."

"Sure," replied Cliff softly. "One of my accounts is a design engineering company. They design large custom power plants for their clients all over the world. They finished a big one in China this year."

From Cliff's demeanor, Charlie felt Cliff was a High S.

"Our competition didn't mind talking about their new products," Cliff continued. "They categorized our product line as dated and soon to be obsolete. You all know that's not true, but because I wasn't even talking about future directions with the head of development, they didn't consider us for the China project. The deal was worth $300,000."

The Agile Manager spoke. "That was a difficult situation for Cliff. Cynthia, I think you experienced something similar last week at Acme Labs. Would you please tell us what happened?"

Cynthia had a High C or Conscientiousness-style personality. She thought for a moment and then nodded her head. "Yes, the situation was similar. Our competition was providing inaccurate information about our products. I learned of this from one of our inside supporters who thought their tactics were inappropriate."

Paul again interrupted, "Well, what did you do, Cindy?"

"Paul, it's Cynthia—not Cindy. I set up a meeting with their technical staff and presented the details on our products. This data cleared up the inaccurate information the competition was spreading and he lost credibility as a result. I don't think he'll be a factor at this account for a while."

"Thanks Cynthia," said the Agile Manager. "The difference between these two similar situations was that Cynthia got word of the competition's activity inside the account and Cliff did not. This a good reminder to us all on the importance of having multiple-level relationships with our customers. Then we have other eyes and hears to keep track of the competition."

"Charlie, is there anything else you want to add?" asked the Agile Manager.

"No, you made your point," replied Charlie. "You can never have enough contacts inside an account. I learned that the hard way myself many years ago."

"Thanks for your input and guidance Charlie," said the Agile Manager. "And thanks to all of you for your willingness to share your experiences. I think we can learn from each other and that will help us all to be successful. Now, if anyone is hungry, dinner is on me and Charlie is our guest of honor."

Afterwards, the Agile Manager reflected upon what a good coaching session this was for the team. People participated actively, they benefited from a "back-to-basics" discussion from a successful peer, and they learned from their mistakes.

The Agile Manager's Checklist

✔ For better and faster results, adapt your coaching style to the person you're coaching.

✔ People generally fall into four categories:

    High D's like action, opportunity, and challenges.

    High i's are talkers who like to get results through people.

    High S's are team players who always meet deadlines.

    High C's are sticklers for detail who like to operate under known standards and written instructions.

Chapter Three

Create the Right Motivational Environment

"As I grow older, I pay less attention to what people say. I just watch what they do."

ANDREW CARNEGIE

The Agile Manager was very excited about announcing an employee incentive program that would reward outstanding individual performance. It had been in the planning stages for several months and, with the help of an outside incentive company, he was finally in a position to roll it out.

The Agile Manager had sensed that the morale throughout the organization could use a boost. He was confident that this new program would do the trick and have a positive impact on every employee.

The Agile Manager identified criteria by which to measure performance for all the positions in key departments throughout the organization. On a monthly basis, he would announce the best performer in each position within a department. They'd be rewarded with great prizes they could pick from a fantastic gift catalog. The catalog selections included weekend getaways, home furnishings, clothing, jewelry, electronic equipment, and more. Each department winner was also going to be recognized in the company's monthly electronic newsletter.

The Agile Manager was looking forward to reviewing the results each month. He expected an across-the-board increase in performance and productivity as a result of the program.

The prizes were so exciting that the Agile Manager was convinced the people would go all out to win.

But he was disappointed when reviewing the first month's results. Surprisingly, they showed that about half the employees improved their performance somewhat, and about 10 percent improved it significantly. However, the program seemed to have little or no impact on the remaining employees.

The Agile Manager suspected that things would get better the next two months. It was still early. The word was still getting out there. Every employee would seek to achieve top honors in their department. No doubt!

He was wrong. It seemed as though the same employees who tried to excel in order to win the first month were the exact same names that rose to the top the following two months. The Agile Manager noted that although no employees were negligent or not doing their jobs well, a good number simply didn't seem to be motivated by the incentive program. This left him both puzzled and disappointed. Why wasn't every employee stretching to win the prizes and accolades that went with them?

People are different. They are different in physical appearance, how they act or react, mannerisms, speech patterns, feelings, beliefs, and motivations—just to name a few.

From a distance, snowflakes may all appear to be similar, but no two are exactly alike. The same is true for people—your employees. The individuals on your team are truly unique.

A strong motivational drive is already present in most of your people. It is up to us as managers or coaches to channel this drive to achieve desired results. Even the best leaders cannot, in the strict sense of the word, motivate their people. What they can do is help people motivate themselves by creating the right motivational climate.

Let a Thousand Flowers Bloom

It is possible that some of you may be wondering why you need to adapt your style to the person. After all, you're the boss, right? People are supposed to obey you, right? There probably was a time and a place for a management style that leaned more toward "my way or the highway," but it's long gone. Over time, effective managers learn that their people are a lot more productive when they treat each person the way they would prefer to be treated.

A satisfier or motivator to one person may be a dissatisfier or demotivator to another. It is important for us as managers to understand the motivational factors that influence our people so they can realize their full potential and produce maximum results.

> **Best Tip**
>
> Understand that all people are motivated. But they are motivated for their own reasons, so you need to get to know them—and well.

It's safe to say that all people are motivated. However, they are motivated for their own reasons and not ours. Given that there are positive and negative motivators for different people, there is no single best motivational pattern or environment for us to try to create.

Get to Know Your People

It's important for you to become familiar with the people within your organization.

Being familiar with them requires an investment of time and effort. But the knowledge and understanding of your people you gain will be the foundation for creating a motivational climate that maximizes performance. You'll begin to understand how to bring out the best effort of each team member.

Help People Reach Goals

Getting to know your people includes becoming aware of their personal goals. If possible, help those goals become a reality.

Say one of your team members wants to move into management one day. You can help by providing opportunities to hone skills. Or you can help by encouraging the person to take a specific course at a local community college.

Sometimes, you help by counseling: "Mary, I understand you eventually want to become a programmer, and I respect that. You're like me in that you're not the most technically oriented person around here. For you to get what you want will require you to be disciplined and focused. I'll do what I can to help guide you. The challenge is significant, but if you really want it badly enough I know you'll work hard at it. Let's explore some next steps . . ."

Best Tip

Motivate those of the Dominance Style by throwing out challenges and giving them control of the situation.

Your assistance doesn't always have to have a direct impact on a situation. Sometimes this is unavoidable, such as when you don't have enough "clout" to help directly. In that case, your role may come in the form of moral support and encouragement.

Occasionally, for example, you may act as a sounding board for members of your team. That may be all they need—someone they respect who'll listen to them.

At the end of the day, you'll feel rewarded by helping people reach their goals. Furthermore, they'll remember you with respect, and some will follow the same path themselves when managing others.

Tailor Your Coaching

Deal with people fairly and consistently. Yet at the same time recognize that individual behavioral styles demand individual approaches to help them perform at peak levels.

Let's look again at the four major types of behavioral styles: Dominance, Influence, Steadiness, and Conscientiousness. It is wise for us to recognize each of these styles, understand their individual needs, and tailor our coaching style to the situation. When you attempt to genuinely satisfy the needs of an individual, you'll interest them in becoming an active contributor to your team.

Note: You find people of all types in all kinds of jobs. Don't assume, for instance, that the accounting guy down the hall is Conscientiousness personified. He may be, in fact, a High D (Dominance).

Motivate the Dominance Style

People of the Dominance Style, recall, like to control their environment by overcoming opposition to accomplish desired results. They enjoy moving people around in their favor.

They are direct, forceful, impatient, and opinionated. They enjoy being in charge, making decisions, solving problems, and getting things done. They tend to thrive on power, prestige, and authority, and they can be extremely

> **Best Tip**
>
> Motivate those of the Influence Style by giving them lots of your time and by tying your goals to their dreams.

demanding. They also fear being taken advantage of by losing control of a situation.

When people of this style are negatively motivated, they can become defiant. They don't like being told what to do, and win-lose challenges can be dangerous.

For example, giving them work that involves dealing with lots of detail would be tedious and demotivating for High D's. They would quickly become bored with a routine that was basically the same from day to day, particularly if it didn't allow them to make decisions that would hinder their desire to be in control.

To create the right motivational environment for such people:

- Be clear, direct, and to the point when you interact.
- Avoid being too personal or talking too much about non-work items.

- Let them know what you expect of them. If you must direct them, provide choices that give them the opportunity to make decisions to satisfy their need to be "in control."
- Accept their need for variety and change. When possible, provide new challenges, as well as opportunities to direct the efforts of others.

The High D person is motivated by personal control through direct communication. Compliment them for results they achieve. They are "bottom line" oriented. Ask them about their career plans and timetables for achieving success. Show how *they* can get results by helping *you* get results.

Motivate the Influence Style

People with this style try to shape the environment by influencing or persuading others to see things their way. They really enjoy being involved with people and getting recognition for their accomplishments. They fear rejection or loss of social approval. They may have a dislike for handling complex details or working as "lone rangers." They prefer to deal with people rather than things.

This highly social individual loves opportunities to verbalize thoughts, feelings, and ideas. So provide opportunities for them to do this when possible. When it's deserved, praise their work enthusiastically and publicly.

When you negatively motivate people of this style, they can be indiscriminately impulsive. When this happens, they may speak first and think later with little regard for what they say and who might hear it. This can be in the form of complaining to no one in particular while hanging around the coffee pot.

Because they want to be liked, being silent or tight-lipped with them will make them afraid you're rejecting them.

Such people run well with new ideas. Take advantage of the strong communication skills that this style possesses by allowing them to be the liaison with other departments when there's a companywide initiative that suits their talents.

They can also be among your best promoters for new ideas or for creating excitement for company social functions such as holiday parties. Because of their desire to be involved with other people and in different projects simultaneously, this style could benefit by receiving time and priority support from you as their coach.

You'll need to communicate more with people of this style, and it'll often involve social interaction. To that end:

- Give them lots of your time.
- Compliment them.
- Ask about things going on in their lives outside of work.
- Let them share with you their goals at work and elsewhere.
- Tie your objectives to their dreams and goals.

Motivate the Steadiness Style

The Steadiness behavioral type focuses on cooperating with others to carry out the task. These people are very much team players and cooperative group workers. They take pride in being reliable and trustworthy employees.

They tend to be patient, loyal, and resistant to sudden changes in their environment. They respond positively to group achievement recognition, sincere appreciation and predictable situations. When they get negatively motivated—which is often caused by sudden, unplanned changes that they see as high risk—they can become stubborn or stern, moods usually expressed in the form of passive resistance.

Best Tip

To motivate those of the Steadiness Style, avoid sudden changes and praise their contributions to the team.

This type of behavioral style responds very well to an atmosphere of cooperation rather than competition. Show sincere appreciation when it's earned. Communicate in an indirect, casual style. Recognize and praise contributions to the team. Schedule regular performance reviews.

To create a positive climate for people using the Steadiness Style:

- Acknowledge that their efforts help others. Provide opportunities for them to cooperate with others on the team to achieve desired results.
- Provide specific direction and offer assurances when necessary.
- When implementing change, be sure to lay out a systematic, step-by-step procedure and draw out their concerns and worries about the situation. They need to feel secure.
- Assure them that you've thought things through before initiating changes. Give them a plan to deal with problems when they occur.

Motivate the Conscientiousness Style

This style emphasizes working conscientiously within existing circumstances to ensure quality and accuracy. People of this behavioral style appreciate opportunities for thorough, careful planning. They are critical thinkers who are sticklers for detail. They prefer to spend time analyzing a situation and, like the steadiness style, are slow to accept sudden changes. They like following procedures and standards—preferably their own.

One of their greatest fears is criticism of their work or efforts. Provide them with:

- Opportunities to demonstrate their expertise.
- Plenty of details.
- Enough time to prepare for meetings properly—especially if they have an item on the agenda to present.
- Situations where their systematic approach will contribute to long-term success.

When they are negatively motivated they may become cynical or overly critical. They will normally respond well to logical, well-thought-out, planned options. Be realistic and avoid exaggeration in discussion with them. They respond favorably to exact job descriptions and performance objectives, scheduled performance appraisals, and specific feedback on their performance.

Your conversations with them will take longer because they'll

probably have several questions. They'll also want to verify the quality and reliability of information you give them. Even when given all the facts, they are inclined to analyze an issue and de-
cide for themselves. Compliment them for the quality work they do, as well as the logical approach they take to doing it.

Best Tip
To motivate those of the Conscientiousness Style, provide lots of details and opportunities to show their expertise.

The Agile Manager analyzed why some people responded favorably to the opportunity to be a star within their departments, while others had little desire for that recognition.

He discovered something interesting. The people who didn't respond by performing at a higher level tended to have many of the characteristics of the Steadiness Style. It occurred to him that perhaps they were uncomfortable competing with other people within their own departments. He decided to test his theory.

For the next quarter, the Agile Manager added another category that recognized and rewarded outstanding performance by work teams.

Bingo. Quarterly results showed that contributions made by the employees with the Steadiness Style improved and contributed greatly to the outstanding performance of the department as a whole. Individual acknowledgement or rewards weren't important to these people. What was? The opportunity to cooperate with others on the team to help the group gain notoriety.

The Agile Manager learned an important lesson that wouldn't soon be forgotten: Different strokes for different folks!

Mix 'em Up

If you can, mix behavior styles on your team so you have people with all four styles. This can make for an effective work team, because each style brings a strength to the table. Mixing will net you greater results as the team gains strength through diversity.

In putting together a diverse group, you'll have a challenge in trying to minimize interpersonal conflicts. Yet your team can achieve your desired results if certain conditions exist. Set a positive tone in these areas:

- Mutual respect.
- Mutual trust.
- Recognition and acceptance that people are different.
- Adaptability in your coaching style to create an atmosphere that allows people to motivate themselves. You have to have the skill and, more importantly, the will to be the effective Agile Manager.

On the way home after a staff meeting his boss held, the Agile Manager reflected on the reasons why they always lasted so long. They started precisely on time but were never scheduled to end at a specific time. This one lasted over six hours—wrapping up at eight in the evening.

The Agile Manager recognized that these sessions tended to follow the same pattern, with the boss monopolizing much of the meeting. Afterwards, the six other participants, including the Agile Manager, felt beat up, exhausted, and emotionally, mentally, and physically drained.

The Agile Manager thought about the other managers in the group. Three had the Influence Style, two were Steadiness types, and one used the Conscientiousness Style.

The boss, a combination of the Conscientiousness and Dominance Styles, was predictable in the behavior he exhibited to the team.

At the meetings, each area manager presented his or her status report for key initiatives. People asked questions or commented during the presentations. The boss—wanting to satisfy the need to be in control—would fire "Why?" questions at the presenter.

The boss's Conscientiousness side would digest the answer. If it lacked the details, facts, and logic this type wanted, bang! It activated and energized the Dominance side. This side was direct, demanding, and determined to control the environment.

On many occasions, the Agile Manager reflected, only the staff member with the Conscientiousness Style would escape unscathed. She was naturally inclined to overanalyze and research all possible options in search of the best available solution or recommendation—even when the project wasn't worth the effort.

If the boss disagreed and went into his "in your face" mode, she withdrew totally. Her whole physical makeup changed drastically as she clammed up in her protective shell.

The others on the staff felt it was impossible to please the boss. One of the Agile Manager's cohorts admitted, "I've learned it doesn't really matter how much I prepare. I'm going to get humiliated anyway, so why devote lots of time preparing?"

The Agile Manager recognized that while he couldn't do anything about his boss's de-

Best Tip

To strengthen your work group, make sure it includes people of all the personality styles.

motivating behavior, he could put his staff at ease at the meetings he presided over. He recognized that the "one style fits all" form of management didn't create the right motivational climate for all team members. Like a professional football quarterback, who calls an "audible" at the line of scrimmage to maximize effectiveness, The Agile Manager was adaptable in interacting with the people on his staff. He treated them all fairly and in a manner that allowed them to motivate themselves.

The Agile Manager's mind drifted back to last week's staff meeting. His marketing manager, who used the Influence Style, said, "I have a great new idea that I'd like to share with all of you." She told all about a new campaign to keep existing customers loyal to the company.

While her excitement was contagious and all delighted in her ability to present the "big picture," it also was obvious that the plan was lacking attention to detail in some important areas. The Agile Manager bit his lip and let her continue to share her ideas hoping that his concerns would be addressed before she finished.

He wasn't disappointed. "Of course, I recognize that I have lots of loose ends with my thought process on this—particularly with regards to some of the nitty-gritty implementation detail. But that is where I thought Joe and Pat could help me out since it is an area of strength for them."

The Agile Manager simply sat back with great pleasure as these two members of his team, both possessing the Steadiness Style, gladly filled in the missing pieces of the puzzle by addressing how to proceed.

The Agile Manager's Checklist

✔ Remember that different things motivate different people. Understanding personality styles is a key to understanding how to motivate people.

✔ Help people reach their personal goals whenever you can. It'll help you reach yours sooner.

✔ Never assume that certain professions are populated by particular personality types. You'll find all types in all jobs.

✔ On teams of diverse personalities, set a constructive tone by modeling respect, trust, acceptance of people's differences, and adaptability.

Chapter Four

Set Goals and Communicate Expectations

*"Whatever the mind of man can conceive
and believe, it can achieve."*

NAPOLEON HILL IN *THINK AND GROW RICH*

One Friday afternoon, the Agile Manager and one of his newly appointed supervisors were having lunch at a favorite spot for pizza. They bantered lightheartedly over sodas while waiting for their pizza to arrive.

Upon finishing a short joke, the supervisor turned serious: "Would it be OK if we talk about a problem I'm having with one of the people in my department?" The Agile Manager nodded approvingly.

"During my first three months as a supervisor, things have gone along smoothly. They still pretty much are except for my interactions with one of my people—Jamie."

"What seems to be the problem?" the Agile Manager asked.

"Well, you recall Jamie is one of the people allowed to work from home since there is no branch office for hundreds of miles. This has really created some challenges for me."

The Agile Manager said, "Tell me more about these challenges—are we talking about performance issues?"

"No, not really performance issues. In fact, that's part of the challenge I'm facing. Jamie's performance has actually been consistently on target. So far, she's exceeded the majority of goals and objectives for that position."

"So what seems to be the problem?"

"It's possible I'm making a mountain out of a molehill, but there are some things that I expect people in these remote locations to do on a regular basis so that I can stay on top of things." The Agile Manager just nodded and continued to listen.

"In order to try to communicate effectively, I've asked these people to call me once a day—or more if they have any situations to discuss. I've also given them the option of either sending me an e-mail or a voice mail at the end of every work day that outlines their activities for the day, progress with specific accounts, and any action items or loose ends that need to be followed up on and resolved."

"All the people on my team have been doing a good job communicating this way except for Jamie."

"Well, what's happening there?" asked the Agile Manager.

"Communication from Jamie is spotty at best. I pretty much get a telephone call during the day but there have been weeks when I received only two or three e-mail or voice-mail messages and it's really driving me crazy. If everybody else can be conscientious enough to contact me at the end of every day, I can't see why Jamie has to be different."

"Have you talked to Jamie about this?"

"I mentioned something a month or so ago and kind of made a joke out of it. From a performance standpoint, Jamie is doing a good job, so maybe I am overreacting. But it really is bothering me. I find that I can do a better job assisting the other people with situations they're dealing with because of the end-of-the-day messages I receive from them. They usually have to give them some thought and analyze their own activities. I find lots of merit in them doing that and in me staying on top of what is happening."

The Agile Manager looked intently at the young supervisor

and asked, "So when do you intend to bring this up with Jamie?"

"That's why I am talking to you. I'm not exactly sure how to handle it. Again, I'm very happy with her performance. But who knows—it could conceivably be even better if I had an opportunity to look at a situation and maybe offer a fresh perspective."

With that the pizza was served by a friendly waiter with a big smile and cheery, "Here it is—our famous thin-crusted specialty. Just the way you like it."

There were a few minutes of silence as each took a slice and began eating. The Agile Manager was thinking, "Hmmm. I really like this pizza and I think I better try to help my supervisor before a real problem develops."

One of the keys to being an effective coach and leader is the ability to set realistic goals for yourself and the members of your team, and then communicate your goals and expectations to subordinates, associates, peers, and superiors.

When people on the team don't know exactly what is expected of them, they're not able to achieve high levels of performance. Then you become disappointed, and the people on your team become frustrated because things do not go as expected.

Best Tip

Make sure people understand and accept your goals. Then make sure they commit themselves to meeting expectations.

Setting goals and communicating expectations effectively also helps to improve the interpersonal climate for you and your people. It greatly reduces the need for confronting poor performers. Why? Because problems with performance often arise when you communicate your expectations ineffectively. That's right—poor performance in others often begins with *you*.

Moreover, don't assume that people understand goals and expectations. Have them acknowledge that they understand, accept, and commit to reaching those goals and meeting expectations.

Now is a good time for you to pause and consider a few questions:

1. What are a few of your important business goals?
2. When were these goals set?
3. Have they been updated?
4. What are a few of your people's business goals?
5. Do your business goals and your people's goals complement or conflict with one another?
6. Do all the people on your team know what your business goals are?
7. Do you know what their goals are?
8. How did you learn theirs and how did they learn yours?
9. Do all members of your team know what is expected of them in detail?
10. How and when did you communicate this?
11. Did they "buy in" to these goals? How do you know?

Put this book aside and answer these questions now. It's the starting point for the discussion that follows.

Manage Yourself

Before we talk about how to set goals, one thing: The example you set for your people has a direct impact on their motivation, performance, and job satisfaction. Effective managers genuinely enjoy their work because they accomplish more and take the time to "smell the roses" or reward themselves.

You can help your team achieve top performance levels by improving your self-management capabilities. That starts with setting both personal and business goals.

Set the Right Goals

In setting goals for individual members of your team and the team as a whole, it's important to keep in mind the goals that your boss has set.

For example, if your boss tells you your team should produce 100 widgets each day, set your team goal slightly higher than

---

FIVE SUCCESS PRINCIPLES

1. Success comes to those who are motivated from within to achieve high goals.

2. Success is a journey—not a destination—that is shared by people who work hard with a positive mental attitude.

3. Success in human endeavor requires practice, practice, practice.

4. Work becomes fun, not an unpleasant means of paying bills, when we set and achieve specific goals.

5. We can turn adversity into opportunity if we think with a positive mental attitude.

6. To achieve anything worthwhile in life, we must have a positive mental attitude no matter what other successful attributes we possess. A positive mental attitude is the energy that, combined with several other attributes, allows us to reach our goals.

---

that—perhaps 110 widgets. Naturally, individual goals for each team member should allow you the opportunity to hit that number of 110. That will make both you, your boss, and the members of your team all very happy.

The point is, don't just go about setting goals haphazardly. Your objective is to set the right goals, based in part on your organization's expectations of you. If you don't know what these expectations are, have your boss spell them out.

Here are four tips for setting useful goals:

1. Don't try to keep your goals in your head; write them down. Be positive. State what you want to do. If you want to avoid or stop doing something, state your goal in terms of what you want to do instead. For example, don't have a goal like, "The organization won't lose money in the second half of the year." Instead, state the goal in a positive fashion, and with greater specificity. "The organization will show a profit of $740,000 for the second half of the year."

2. Be specific. It is important that you are able to measure your progress as you work toward your goal. The more specific your goal, the easier it is to measure your progress. Always quantify your goal. Your goal statement should answer as many of the following questions as possible in order to be specific:

—Who?
—What?
—When?
—Where?
—To what extent?
—How?
—How much?
—How long?
—How hard?

3. Make sure goals are achievable and yet require a "stretch" to reach them. Setting unrealistically high goals will dissatisfy you and your people, because you'll never quite reach your objective. Worse, some of your people might not even try to get there. It is better to set smaller goals, meet them, and then step up to a higher goal.

4. Set deadlines—they provide the needed time for achieving your goal. Deadlines also give you something to aim for.

Example: Our goal is for each member of the team to sell at least $500,000 of new products and services at an existing account by the end of the fiscal year. We will achieve this goal by conducting interviews with all members of senior management at the account to clearly understand their needs and propose solutions that help them realize their objectives.

Goals + the Right Activities = Success

Sometimes people focus only on the results they want to achieve without regard for the activities necessary to get there.

Unfortunately, there are also people who focus only on activities. This usually happens because goals have not been clearly stated.

Effective people follow a goal-setting process and then decide what activities are necessary to get them there.

As you can see, the example above emphasizes *doing something*. It describes what activities will lead to accomplishing the goal.

Achieve Large Goals Through Small Steps

In the goal example just noted, the most difficult part of this goal (or any other goal) is getting started. The organization can't accomplish this particular goal until:

- It ensures consistent support for current customers;
- It identifies target accounts and opportunities;
- It creates interest through interview appointments that identify senior management's important needs and goals;
- It presents an attractive proposition to the customer;
- It gains commitment and closes the sale.

You achieve large goals, then, through a series of smaller steps:

1. Ensuring current customer support is satisfactory.
2. Evaluating the account base to identify your best new product opportunities.
3. Calling on senior management to set appointments.
4. Identifying senior management's needs and goals.
5. Demonstrating the true value of your new products and services.
6. Presenting an attractive proposition that adds value.
7. Gaining commitment to close the sale.

Each step has a specific objective. They are what you and the individuals on your team would expect to accomplish. Objectives are the results you are looking for from each step. Think of objectives as mini-goals.

Just as with your overall goal, you should be able to answer as many of these questions as possible for these mini-goals:

1. Who?
2. Will do what?
3. Where? In what situation?
4. How much? To what degree?
5. By when?

Do this for each step required to reach your goal.

"How are you enjoying lunch?" asked the Agile Manager. Caught with a mouthful of food, the supervisor just smiled and nodded quickly to indicate that the pizza hit the spot. "Good, I'm glad. Let me tell you a story that I think might help with the situation. Before you moved here from Northern California you enjoyed your 49ers season tickets—didn't you?"

The supervisor smiled and said, "Oh, you bet. I still have fond memories of winning all those Super Bowls."

The Agile Manager enjoyed the enthusiastic response of the supervisor and added, "I bet you did. Unfortunately, around here we haven't had that opportunity even once. We've had many head coaches come and go for lots of reasons, but the last coach we had probably left town due to a communication problem not unlike your situation with Jamie."

The supervisor didn't bother to pick up another slice of pizza. Instead he focused completely on the Agile Manager's words. "This coach made significant progress by bringing in new talent and putting together a team that was able to make the playoffs three years in a row. Nevertheless, that head coach failed to get his contract renewed at the end of the initial term, and I don't think it had anything to do with on-field performance."

"Really?" said the young supervisor. "What could be more important than on-field performance?"

"Well, certainly wins and losses are something that every owner pays close attention to. But I think this franchise's owner was also very image conscious. The image that the team had, which by the way was not only allowed but encouraged by the head coach, was that of a wild bunch of renegades out of control both on and off the field. It was the off-the-field antics that not only annoyed the owner but caused him to have repeated

THE SUCCESS PROCESS

1. Prioritize your goals and note what activities are necessary to achieve them.

2. Break each of your goals into a series of small steps necessary to reach that goal.

3. Arrange the steps required into a logical sequence.

4. Set specific objectives for each of the steps.

5. Reach objectives by following the goal-setting guidelines: Be specific. Be positive. Set a deadline.

6. Be realistic. Set objectives you and your people can meet if you stretch. When you meet that objective, go on to the next. Achieving each objective creates momentum.

7. As key objectives and goals are met, don't forget to reward yourself and your people.

shouting matches with the head coach." The Agile Manager smiled. "Of course, this particular head coach had no problem matching decibel levels with the owner."

The supervisor asked, "So how does this relate to my situation with Jamie?"

"That's a good question. This head coach was here for five years, and his lax discipline with the players began immediately. Rumor has it that the owner let the situation eat away at him for the first three years without saying a word to the coach. I guess it was like a volcano building up. Then, in year four, the shouting matches started. The volcano erupted. Go ahead and have another slice of pizza. It's going to get cold," said the Agile Manager.

As the supervisor ate, the Agile Manager continued, "I think the coach and the owner were on the same page when it came to the performance goals for the team. I'm sure they had both hoped to achieve at least ten wins and reach the playoffs and make progress from year to year in the playoffs—all of which the team did. But beyond setting and communicating goals, I think there is an important step that the owner failed to do."

"What was that?" asked the supervisor.

"Clearly communicate his expectations that the coach and the members of the team conduct themselves appropriately as representatives of the city and the franchise."

"The longer those expectations were not met, and the longer the owner didn't bring it up with the coach, the worse the situation became. Although on-field performance improved from year to year, the image of the team within the community deteriorated. The owner should have done a more effective job clearly communicating the expectations he had of the organization. And then, just as importantly, when those expectations weren't being met, he would have been better off to talk to the coach in the first year rather than let three seasons go by and then have a big blow up."

They left the restaurant and headed back to the office without saying a word for the first few minutes. Then the supervisor spoke: "This story has really helped me realize that I could be turning a small problem into a huge problem by not effectively communicating my expectations to everyone on my team. If I don't talk to Jamie about this now, things will only get worse. It's going to continue to eat at me. Besides, it's possible that I could help improve Jamie's already good performance. I think what I need to do is again state what my expectations are and the value of those expectations being met."

They had reached the building and the Agile Manager turned toward the supervisor saying, "I wouldn't wait until tomorrow to do that. Don't blow things out of proportion or overstate and therefore complicate the situation with Jamie. But my advice is to be clear, concise, direct, and to the point. Be sure you also gain agreement from Jamie that you can count on receiving those end-of-day messages on a daily basis. Getting that commitment from Jamie is important. Without it you're assuming that your expectations are clearly understood and will be met. It's starting to rain. Let's get back inside."

Communicate Expectations

By now, the expectations you have of your people should be clear—to you.

Naturally, it's equally important that your people know what your expectations are. Ineffective managers often fail to communicate expectations. Instead, they communicate goals only.

For example, a monthly output goal should also have expectations that help guarantee you achieve it. Depending on the situation, you may expect that a certain daily or weekly report be generated, reviewed, and acted on if necessary. Or, during peak times for a seasonal business, you may expect that a smaller percentage of people take vacation time than normally would, and that some people will need to work overtime.

Whatever your expectations are, they are useless unless you communicate them properly. To do that, take these steps:

Step 1: *Identify your expectations.* This is different than goal setting. Here you want to focus on all those activities you feel are required to achieve goals as well as any others that are important to you. In that regard, you may also want to identify some ground rules for the team. In professional sports, for instance, team members are expected to wear uniforms, and with their shirttails tucked in. Players may also be expected to be available to the press after a game.

Step 2: *Communicate those expectations to your people.* How you do this depends on the situation. You can communicate one on one, or in a group setting. Some expectations are best communicated in writing after you first deliver them verbally. Use common sense. If an expectation is important, don't take shortcuts in communicating it.

Best Tip

When setting goals, don't forget an all-important step: Chart the specific activities that will help you and your team reach them.

Step 3: *Be certain people understand the expectations, clarify-*

ing any areas necessary. Don't assume things are clear to everyone. Give your people an opportunity to ask questions.

Step 4: *Be sure to gain acknowledgment and commitment from all members of your team.* How this is best accomplished will depend on circumstances.

If you are setting expectations for someone who has not lived up to previous commitments, for example, it makes sense to put your expectations in writing and to get the person to sign off in acknowledgment of them. After setting expectations in a team meeting, you might say, "Unless anyone has any questions, it's my understanding I have everyone's commitment on this." Wait for questions before concluding the point: "Good. Thank you. Let's move on . . ."

We would suggest that it is also extremely worthwhile for you as the manager or coach to understand what expectations your people have of you as their leader.

No one goes to work to fail intentionally. All of your people want to be successful at what they do. Create, therefore, an atmosphere that encourages your team members to let you know what they expect of you as their manager and coach.

How do you do that? Make it easy—ask them! An employee's expectations of you may include things like: leadership, honesty,

---

Coaching Tip:
HOW TO HAVE AN EFFECTIVE MEETING

- Gather all your people together and communicate your expectations to them.
- Go around the room and have the members of your team tell you what their expectations of you are as their manager or coach.
- Write these down on a white board or flip chart.
- Distribute the list to everyone shortly after the meeting in written format.

tools to be effective, open communication, direction when needed, or help in reaching personal goals related to their careers.

Communicate Expectations the Holtz Way

We've had several opportunities to learn about the philosophy of Coach Lou Holtz regarding the importance of setting and communicating goals and expectations. He stresses the significance of writing down goals, making sure they are realistic—while always aiming high—and having a solid plan of action to get to each goal. He also believes that goals can build upon one another.

In the mid-1980s, Holtz took over the reigns as the head football coach at the University of Notre Dame and immediately went about setting and communicating his goals:

1. National Championship
2. Play in a January 1st Bowl Game
3. Finish the Season Among the Top Ten–Ranked Teams in the Country
4. Play in a Post-Season Bowl Game
5. Have a Winning Season

Notice that Holtz always had another goal to shoot for if one of the higher ones became unattainable as the season went on.

As for effectively communicating his expectations as to how these goals could be accomplished, Holtz began by sending a simple message using two words joined together on the front of a T-shirt that each player wore during workouts:

TEAMe

Holtz communicated other expectations, of course, but this brief, concise, to-the-point message is notable. By the way, that National Championship goal was achieved in just a few short seasons.

Understand Why People Don't Do What You Expect Them To

It can be frustrating for any manager or coach to have people on the team fail to do what is expected of them. Let's take a look at some examples and their probable causes.

Problem	Possible Cause
1. They don't know why they should do it.	*Poor communication.*
2. They don't know how to do it.	*Lack of skill or training.*
3. They don't know what is expected.	*Don't understand or poor communication.*
4. They are afraid to try something new.	*Afraid of consequences.* *Lack of confidence—they think they can't.* *Fear of failure or fear of success.*
5. They think they have a better way to do it.	*They'd rather stay within their comfort zone.* *Maybe they do have a better way.*
6. Something else has priority.	*Shortcomings and time-management skills.*
7. Not interested in a reward if they do it.	*Insignificant reward or nothing "extra."*
8. They think they're doing what you wanted.	*Lack of communication.* *Incorrect feedback.*
9. They are rewarded for not doing it.	*Failure to confront them.* *Giving your permission to continue.*
10. They get punished for doing what they are supposed to do.	*Insensitive communication.* *Peer pressure.*
11. Obstacles beyond their control.	*Little or no resources.* *Barriers preventing performance.*

12. Personal limitations.	*They don't belong in the job.*
	Lack of aptitude or
	organization.
	Not interested in the work or
	assignment.
13. Personal problems.	*Emotional.*
	Personal business.
	Poor attitude or very low
	commitment.
14. No one can do it.	*Unrealistic expectations.*
	It's never been done before.

This is a short list. You can add to it based on your own personal experiences.

Making sure that your people clearly understand what is expected will benefit you in many ways including:

A. You'll be disappointed less frequently.

B. People not meeting your expectations won't be surprised when you have to confront them.

Now let's take a look at some things that you can do to make sure that your people do what is expected. A number of these will help you avoid some of the problems listed above, or as ways you can address them effectively as they arise.

1. Communicate all your expectations. Let your people know what is expected of them. Whenever it's mission critical, put it in writing. Don't simply assume that you have a person's commitment—ask for it.

2. Make sure they know how to do whatever it is you want them to do. Ask questions and listen to their answers. Provide feedback as needed and training if required.

3. Whenever possible, explain the logic or reasons behind doing something. Always try to avoid just issuing orders. Draw out their concerns and provide feedback.

4. When appropriate, offer possible approaches for accomplishing the needed results.

5. Listen to their ideas and allow them to try a new approach if it's better. Provide feedback.

6. Be certain that they understand your priorities and the timeframe for completion. Leave no doubt in their minds about how you will measure performance.

7. Ask about their concerns and give them reassurance. Provide feedback.

8. Be understanding or empathetic about real personal problems. Have a backup plan ready to implement if necessary.

9. Be sure you're setting realistic expectations and take into consideration resources, skill set, and experience level.

10. Anticipate and discuss possible obstacles and provide a strategy for working around them.

11. Don't hesitate to ask the members of your team for their input. Share solutions and provide feedback!

Try a Performance Contract

There are times when it may be appropriate and more effective to create a "performance contract" with one of the members of your team. This contract is a great way to cement goals and communicate your expectations.

Like any contract, the performance contract can be either verbal or written. Verbal performance contracts are the easier of the two to make and the easiest to break—as you know if you've ever had someone "forget" to do something they committed themselves to doing.

If the situation or behavior style of the person requires it, get a written performance contract. It will be an effective method to use with some team members. Written contracts may seem extreme, but in some circumstances it's the best way to ensure that people will remember to keep their promises.

Written performance contracts can take different forms. They might include a follow-up letter, interoffice memo, or formal agreement of understanding. The agreement should include a review of your discussion and a description of who will do what. We also recommend that you include the following when appropriate:

1. What are you responsible for specifically?

2. What is the person on your team responsible for specifically?

3. What are the concerns, problems, or areas of improvement needed?

4. What do you both require from each other?

5. What are the critical dates involved?

6. When will a progress review take place?

7. What measurement criteria will define success?

8. Both you and your team member should sign and date the performance contract.

Make sure that the written performance contract follows up a prior conversation. It shouldn't catch the individual by surprise. If done effectively, it will serve as a springboard for improved performance.

The idea of a performance contract can also be applied between departments within the same organization. Again, it can be a catalyst for improved cooperation and results.

The Agile Manager was sitting at his dining room table late one night surrounded by papers on which he had written some goals and expectations for the coming fiscal quarter.

He took a sip of coffee and thought that now it was time to take the next step to making these goals become a reality. On a blank sheet of paper, he wrote this question: What can I do to help my people meet the goals and expectations? He wrote down ideas as they came. When the Agile Manager was finished, the list looked this:

1. Measure performance. Provide specific performance feedback often and consistently. Always remember that what gets measured gets done!

2. Reward good performances as it occurs. Verbal feedback is good, written feedback is better.

3. Remove obstacles for my people and/or provide them a way to bypass them.

4. Update my people when priorities change.

5. Eliminate any negative consequences for good performance. Stroke positive performance.

6. Provide "caring confrontation" for negative performance.

7. Use negative consequences (written warnings, performance plans, disciplinary actions, etc.) only for consistent, poor performance.

8. Coach and counsel <u>all</u> my people <u>all</u> the time. Observe them in action as often as possible.

9. Encourage my people to share their experiences. We can learn from both the good ones and also the not-so-good ones.

10. Provide the resources needed in order for each member of my team to be successful.

The Agile Manager's Checklist

✔ Make sure your people know exactly what you expect of them.

✔ Don't assume people understand goals and expectations. Spell them out and make sure they understand and commit to them.

✔ Be specific when setting goals. Ask yourself, "Who, what, where, when, and how?"

✔ Break down large goals into smaller steps or mini-goals.

✔ To best cement goals and communicate expectations, create a performance contract that describes who will do what and when.

Chapter Five

Develop Your People

*"The key to developing people is to catch them
doing something right."*

KEN BLANCHARD AND SPENCER JOHNSON

It was the best of times for the Agile Manager and all other employees to be working at the company. Although in a highly competitive marketplace, the organization had posted improved bottom-line results for twenty consecutive quarters. The senior management team was known never to rest on its laurels and instead consistently looked to the future.

It was with the future in mind that the company decided to acquire a smaller firm strategically positioned to provide a competitive edge. The principal business of the newly acquired company was outside the core business of the Agile Manager's company.

Shortly after the deal was finalized, several people in key positions in the acquired company decided not to remain. As a result, the Agile Manager had to fill an important supervisory slot.

Feeling he had to fill the position quickly, the Agile Manager looked first within the ranks of his own company for a talented individual capable of doing the job. He felt the position called for the type of person who could run things on his or her own—

a self-reliant go-getter to whom he could delegate this responsibility completely.

He gave the job to Kim. She was both excited about the opportunity and confident in her ability to do an outstanding job. The Agile Manager shared that confidence, because Kim had once before been promoted into a supervisory position and been successful.

She had handled that transition with great ease and efficiency. She had initially received regular direction and support from the Agile Manager, but as she became comfortable in her role, direction became unnecessary. Kim had proven herself capable, and the Agile Manager delegated responsibilities completely.

Now, after having been in that supervisory position for three years, both of them were certain the new appointment was the perfect fit. The Agile Manager went so far as to say to Kim, "You've more than proven yourself to be capable of handling a situation like this. We've already discussed the three goals for the short and intermediate term, and I know you'll achieve those. Let me know if there is anything that you need."

The Agile Manager was simply continuing his mode of managing Kim: Give her the objectives and let her do her job.

Neither of them even remotely imagined the difficulty Kim was to have taking over a department in the newly acquired company.

This, Kim realized, was different than becoming a supervisor in her previous job. Then, she was well known, well liked, and respected. In this situation, the employees were still getting adjusted to the idea of working for a different company when their longtime department head decided not to be part of the new organization. It unsettled a large number of them.

Moreover, the employees quickly realized that there was a big difference in management styles between Kim and the previous supervisor. Kim was spontaneous and cared little for details. She often made decisions based on gut instinct and without a great deal of objectivity. Her style worked fine in an environment she truly understood. But in the new job, it helped make a bad situation worse.

Her new staff didn't like her approach to management. And Kim was troubled as well. After all, she relied on the same approach she had always had success with.

After just a few weeks, real problems began to surface. Morale was low, efficiency suffered, and complaints about Kim began to surface both within the department and without.

She was certain she could handle the situation and continued to attack her new responsibilities with great determination and confidence. In fact, at a meeting of supervisors called by the Agile Manager, she didn't feel it was necessary to mention any of her difficulties. She was certain she'd soon get them under control. After all, she thought, "I was put in this position because of my ability to get things done."

Having delegated the responsibility of a smooth transition to Kim, the Agile Manager was extremely late in learning that things in the department weren't going well. In fact, it wasn't until reviewing some reports that clearly indicated a few key objectives were not going to be made that the Agile Manager learned the nature of the situation—four months after putting Kim in charge.

Upon getting this dose of reality, the Agile Manager had many questions. "Why hadn't Kim come to me for assistance? How did this come to be, anyway? Kim had done such a good job in the other department when I delegated things completely to her. What happened to Kim's ability to meet objectives without me having to look over her shoulder? Should I have provided more support? What type of direction did she need that I wasn't giving? How did this go so wrong?"

There is no bigger responsibility, for managers of people, than developing those people to help them realize their maximum potential. Developing people starts the day you first hire them, and the process never stops.

A common formula for managing or coaching your people is to follow the Four *F*'s:

- Be fair,
- Be firm,
- Be frank,
- Be familiar.

In today's world, the most challenging of these is the last.

Being familiar with your people requires time. While it can be challenging to find time, doing so is critical if you want to develop the people on your team.

To be effective in developing your people, versatility (having the skill) and flexibility (having the will) are required. In this chapter, we will recommend proven strategies for gaining the skill and will to groom people in your organization. And these strategies will help you become more familiar with your people—and more valuable to them.

Analyze Your People

It is always wise to analyze the developmental level of each of your people. In today's fast-paced and ever-changing world, your people are often asked to wear different hats and perform various functions. In so doing, you may find them to be highly developed in one or two areas. You may also find them wanting in other areas, depending on things such as experience level, attitude, and the tools they've been given to carry out the responsibilities.

No doubt, the people you manage and coach represent a variety of levels of development. Some may be very experienced and others very inexperienced. You may find that some require a great deal in the way of specific direction and supervision, while others will need you primarily to remove obstacles that may be in their way. For now, take a quick look at the chart at the top of the next page. It offers an overview of developmental levels.

Create a list of the people on your team and their major responsibilities. Then determine each person's present level of development.

You also should take into account the person's behavior style. These behavior styles, as discussed earlier, are:

Style	Driven By
Dominance	Results and Control
Influence	People Involvement and Recognition
Steadiness	Security and Stability
Conscientiousness	Accuracy and Order

Developmental Levels

Level	Strengths & Limitations	Profile	Management/ Coaching Style
Self-reliant	*High competence, high commitment*	*Consistent, top performer*	*Delegate, remove interference, coach*
Independent	*High competence variable commitment*	*Veteran, good performer*	*Support, remove interference, coach*
Intermediate	*Moderate competence, variable commitment*	*Experienced, but erratic performer*	*Remove interference, support, direct, and coach*
Dependent	*Low competence high commitment*	*Rookie, low performer*	*Direct, coach, support, remove interference*

The worksheet might thus consist of name, behavior style, developmental level, and the best coaching and management style. Keep this list handy; it will help you manage and coach more effectively.

Recognize Developmental Levels

Let's take a look at our categories more closely.

Self-Reliant Level. Those at this level are consistently top performers. They always accomplish the task at hand, often beating deadlines and contributing whenever asked to. They exhibit high levels of people skills and technical or job skills. They are self-confident and motivated, and they are willing and able to make decisions on their own. They often "give back" to the organization by helping others on the team.

Independent Level. Those at this level are good, veteran performers with a high level of both people and technical job skills. They do, however, have ups and downs in self-confidence and motivation. The biggest difference between this and the self-reliant level is the lack of consistency.

Intermediate Level. People at this level may be either experienced or inexperienced for the job at hand. But in either case, their performance varies from good to bad. They may also have trouble with self-confidence and motivation. Usually, you wouldn't call such people "self-starters."

Dependent Level. Those at this level are usually new or relatively recent hires performing at low levels as they learn the job. On the plus side, they usually have a strong desire to perform, and they're highly motivated. Nonetheless, they require a great deal of attention.

Adapt Your Coaching Style

Now let's look at how you can deal with each of these types:

Delegate: **Give the person a mission or task and allow him the freedom to decide how to accomplish it.** Delegating is really allowing people to identify, define, manage, and plan most, if not all, of their activities. This style is most effective with people at the self-reliant level. Give them objectives and let them do their job.

Support: **Invest time and create the right motivational climate for each person.** To support, work with the person to identify, define, manage, and plan activities. This style is most effective with people at the independent level. Review their objectives, ask for ideas, and make suggestions—but let them develop their own plans. Review the plan afterwards and periodically. Provide feedback on performance when it's called for.

Supporting also includes time doing things like counseling and stroking. (What's stroking? Think of it as a form of positive reinforcement for a job well done. It's a way of saying "way to go," or "atta boy." You can stroke orally, in writing, or simply by actions like a simple nodding of the head acknowledging approval.)

Direct: **Tell a person exactly what to do and how to do it. Expect no deviations. Look for specific, measurable results.** To direct, give the person an objective and define and prioritize his specific activities. This style is most effective with people at the dependent and intermediate levels. These are your rookies and erratic performers. Review their objectives, ask for input, but give them a specific direction to follow. Always set timetables for them to follow and monitor their progress—daily if necessary. Intensify or lessen your direct involvement depending on their performance.

Coach: **Observe, review, recommend, model, and reward.** This involves reinforcing techniques your people learned in previous training experiences or while on the job.

Coach all your people all the time regardless of their developmental level.

Your style of coaching will vary with your personal development and track record. Focus on proven techniques by reinforcing the principles covered in any previous training attended by your below-average and poor performers.

Coach all your people all the time. Even your best performers can slip once in a while, and they're always ready to learn a few more tricks.

Coach your productive, veteran performers on more advanced skills or areas of their job. Your techniques and involvement will vary depending on their developmental level and behavior style. This particular subject is covered in great detail in the next chapter of this book.

One thought to keep in mind: Newer people, receptive to coaching, are willing to try just about anything they feel will help them. Some veterans, on the other hand, may hesitate to try something new because they fear losing what they already have.

This is a case where being familiar with all members of your team is truly important in helping them realize their maximum potential. Your veteran performers will be much more receptive to a new approach if it's based on sound, firsthand knowledge of them as individuals and the situation that they are in. In this case, familiarity can breed mutual respect.

Remove Interference: **Keep your people productive by removing any and all obstacles that may be in their way and thus limiting performance.** Regardless of the developmental level of a person, strive to remove interference to keep the individual focused and productive. The types of interference or obstacles you need to remove and how you go about it will depend greatly on the individual.

One way to remove potential obstacles for new hires is to have them receive thorough, comprehensive skills training. For someone else on your team, removing interference might involve deploying a particular use of technology to free up time. That will increase their performance levels in mission-critical projects.

Being as familiar as possible with each of the people on your team especially helps in removing the obstacles. That in turn helps them realize their maximum potential.

Take a look at a Coaching/Management Styles Grid on the next page to get a sense of the various levels of development.

As you can see, the levels of direction and support you supply depend on the level of development of the individual at a particular point in time—or for a particular function or a project.

Take Behavioral Style into Account

Someone who is self-reliant requires little direction or support.

Yet it's also important to recognize the behavioral style of the various people on your team. If that self-reliant individual also had the Influence Style, she would require support even though she may be truly self-reliant.

The support would best come in the form of enthusiastic, public praise for her performance. It's also possible that part of your job in removing interference for this individual might include taking care of details or helping her get better organized.

Movement Not Always Upward

In a perfect world, people progress through all four stages of

Coaching/Management Styles Grid

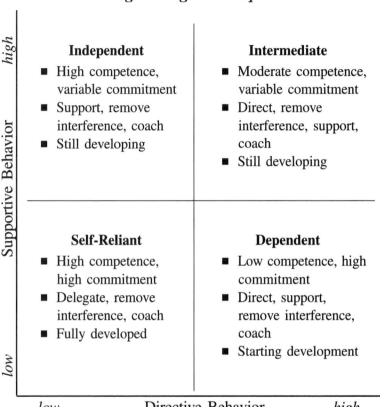

Independent
- High competence, variable commitment
- Support, remove interference, coach
- Still developing

Intermediate
- Moderate competence, variable commitment
- Direct, remove interference, support, coach
- Still developing

Self-Reliant
- High competence, high commitment
- Delegate, remove interference, coach
- Fully developed

Dependent
- Low competence, high commitment
- Direct, support, remove interference, coach
- Starting development

Supportive Behavior — *high* / *low*

low Directive Behavior *high*

development from dependent to self-reliant.

In the real world, your team members will usually move between the stages based on the situation or skill set required for a particular role. As the coach, it's your responsibility to provide the direction, support, or coaching that the situation calls for. You may have to challenge an independent person by giving an assignment with absolutely no direction as a way of developing self-reliance.

Be aware, too, that the competence or commitment that people show is fluid. They can and will move in both directions—progressing towards self-reliance at some points, and regressing at others.

Think of it as you would an investment portfolio—individual stocks go up and down, having an impact on overall performance. It is your challenge to turn around your assets (your people) if they are heading in the wrong direction, while at the same time maximizing the performance of your strong players.

Develop Your Team

Your team isn't self-directed. It's your responsibility to set and clearly communicate goals and objectives. As the team leader, manager, or coach, you have to set the tone and framework for the team's focus, and you have to intervene in situations when necessary.

The basis of the team should be built on mutual trust and respect. Remember, titles do not earn respect; individuals do.

Let's take a look at ten elements that are evident in any effective team.

1. Goal Clarity. Members understand team goals and commit themselves to achieving them. If goals are absolutely clear and you've gained the commitment of a team member, you have earned the right to reward or confront as needed.

2. Recognition/Cooperation. All team members know the strengths of each of the other members and the contributions they bring to the team. All members cooperate with one another and make their own individual contributions to the group.

3. Trust/Support/Cohesiveness. Members have confidence in one another, and they trust and support each other. They aid other team members when problems arise.

4. Role Clarity. Responsibilities and expectations for each team member are clearly spelled out, communicated, and acknowledged. Responsibilities are openly discussed and questions clarified.

5. Means for Solving Role Conflict. Members know what they are supposed to do. Roles complement one another. If they conflict, members discuss and resolve the situation.

6. Participation/Influence/Feedback. Team members express themselves freely in discussions about the job or task at hand.

They are encouraged to participate, and no one discounts ideas. Members recognize the value of open brainstorming.

7. Meeting Effectiveness. Team meetings focus on relevant issues and contribute to the making of sound decisions. Members leave each meeting with a clear understanding of what is expected of them and the team as a whole.

8. Conflict Management. Team members discuss differences of opinion or conflicts openly. Different points of view are discussed until members reach an agreement that makes sense to all members involved. Whenever possible, team members reach a consensus. When that's not possible, you as the leader must make a decision.

9. Energy/Satisfaction. Members feel a sense of accomplishment and satisfaction for their contributions. People know their jobs and work efficiently to get their tasks completed. People have some fun while they work—they know work is more than an unpleasant means to get the bills paid.

10. What's important now! The coach or manager keeps members focused on what's important to be successful now. He or she eliminates unnecessary activities and shelters the team from outside distractions as much as possible.

A year had passed since Kim had been placed in her position by the Agile Manager. Happily, the last six months had seen a marked improvement in the department's performance as a whole. The Agile Manager made note of this in preparing for Kim's annual performance review.

The turnaround certainly didn't happen over night. This was much different than walking into a dark room, hitting the light switch and watching darkness turn to light.

After having analyzed what went wrong during the first four months in her position, the Agile Manager took Kim under his wing for the next sixty days. The first step was for both of them to realize that in her new role she could not be as self-reliant as she had been. Not realizing this to begin with was the mistake—not the fact that she wasn't as self-reliant.

In her new position, in many ways Kim was actually in the dependent stage of development. Her extremely high commitment to the job and the company never wavered, but she had to hone her skills for the new role. Rather than delegating to Kim, the Agile Manager pointed out that he would provide her with more direction for a short period of time and then gradually back off as she became more familiar and comfortable with the situation.

One of the biggest areas of adjustment for her was the need to pay a lot more attention to detail, then to take that information into account before making a decision. Her decisions, said the Agile Manager, needed to be based more on objective than subjective thinking for the time being. Because of her strong desire to succeed in her role and accomplish the results that were needed, she was willing to accept this feedback from the Agile Manager. That commitment actually helped speed up the process to the point where the Agile Manager was able to offer more support and less direction after a few short months.

This experience was a reminder to the Agile Manager of the importance of coaching. It was also an eye-opener. He discovered that our levels of development truly depend on the situation we're in or the task that we're faced with.

The Agile Manager's Checklist

✔ Start developing people the day you hire them—and never stop.

✔ Use these prime coaching tools, depending on the developmental level of the person in question: *delegate, support, direct, coach* (observe and recommend), and *remove obstacles.*

✔ Be aware that people will develop in varying degrees and ways—and can, upon occasion, fall back.

Chapter Six

Coach Hands-On

"It's not whether you get knocked down, it's whether you get up."
VINCE LOMBARDI

Working with your people is a powerful management tool. It allows you to observe them in action performing their jobs. You can compliment their positive actions and immediately coach any actions that need improvement. Approach each coaching opportunity as a one-on-one training session. And remember: Coaching should be done regularly, not just when a person makes a mistake or is in trouble.

Outside of work, the Agile Manager enjoyed many activities. In particular, he loved basketball and had opportunities to coach at various age and talent levels. A few of these opportunities stood out in particular.

Driving into the office one morning, the Agile Manager allowed his mind to drift back over the fifteen years that he had been a volunteer coach. He had once moved into a new city and state and seen a notice in the local community newspaper advertising the need for coaches in a Saturday morning league for children ages eight through ten.

In many ways, the three years that he coached there were the most rewarding, because the majority of the youngsters were learning the fundamentals of the game. The league consisted of teams composed of both boys and girls, who were there to have fun, learn the rules, and learn how to play the game. If they happened to win occasionally, so much the better.

That group of kids was dependent on the coach both in practice sessions and in games.

The Agile Manager chuckled as he recalled one game during his first season coaching this group. He had called one of the youngest players off the bench and instructed him to go into the game to replace one of the other team members. Thrilled to be getting into the action, Steve immediately turned and ran onto the court—without reporting to the scorer's table—shouting, "Pat, it's my turn to play. You have to sit down now" loud enough for everyone in the gym—and within a mile radius— to hear.

With that group you couldn't assume anything as a coach. They needed a great deal of direction. But they had spirit. It reminded the Agile Manager of experiences that he had coaching new recruits in the business world, many of whom were twenty-two year olds in their first jobs. They needed a good deal of direction and would usually be responsive to his coaching, because of their desire to be successful.

When a career move required relocating once again, the Agile Manager was fortunate enough to find another volunteer coaching opportunity for an evening summer league. This group was at a different level of development than his previous team, however. It consisted of teenage boys who played varsity basketball for their high schools.

The other coaches in the league were very competitive, beginning with the player draft. During that first year, the Agile Manager remembered being at a great disadvantage due to his complete lack of knowledge about any of the players in the league.

He remembered in particular picking two players, choices that several of the other coaches found quite amusing at the time. Later on, one of the other coaches mentioned that he and the others avoided those two because one of the players was too selfish and not coachable. "The laughter that followed the other selection," he said, "was probably due to the boy's inability to chew gum and dribble the basketball at the same time."

During the regular season, the Agile Manager had the last laugh as he coached that team to the division championship.

The talent level was far different from the young boys and girls he coached in his old community. Those youngsters, with their raw talent, would hang on the Agile Manager's every word. This group of mostly talented players in his community had to be coached in a different way, because they needed different tools to perform well as a team.

While coaching children, the Agile Manager focused on the basic basketball skills that they had to develop. In coaching high school players, he shifted his attention from fundamentals to coaching more advanced elements of the game—after first having observed and analyzed the performance of each individual. This was not unlike what the Agile Manager found himself doing in today's business environment with the people on his team who had some experience behind them.

Nevertheless, whatever the group, the tremendous enjoyment he received from coaching was the real reward.

During six of the seasons he coached, his teams advanced to the league championship game. That was quite an accomplishment. The league recognized it by naming the coach of the champion team Coach of the Year. Along with that designation went the responsibility for coaching the league's all-star team in competition against other teams throughout the county.

During the week of practices prior to one county tournament, the Agile Manager went about bringing the all-stars together as a team. He observed that each player was highly skilled in the offensive elements of the game. But, in most cases, their defensive capabilities left a lot to be desired. As a result, he focused on fine-tuning their defensive game.

Since they were highly skilled and proud of their accomplishments, the Agile Manager appealed to their desire to become even better in an area where their skills were not as outstanding. In almost every practice session prior to the actual game, the majority of the time was spent working on defense.

The results? The all-star teams they played against usually had a very difficult time scoring. The Agile Manager's team took great pride in holding their opponents to as low a score as possible.

"Enough daydreaming about the past. I better get busy," the Agile Manager said out loud to himself as he returned, mentally, to the present. He hadn't realized how many parallels and comparisons there were between his role as basketball coach and his management position at work.

It really is necessary to coach all your people all the time, he thought. Even the stars. And recognizing each individual's level of development is key to knowing what things to coach them on and how to go about doing it.

As the chart on the opposite page suggests, there are five keys to coaching success. Let's go over them in detail.

1. Observe and Analyze Performance

This is the foundation for all good coaching. In this step, observe the most important activities of your people. Items to consider include:

- Customer interactions (sales interviews, meetings, project implementation, relationship development, problem resolution, etc.)
- Project reporting (timeliness, accuracy, quality/quantity of work)
- Internal paperwork and administration (timeliness, accuracy, quality/quantity)
- Communication skills (internal/external, written, verbal, group or one-on-one interactions)
- Planning (timeliness, accuracy, quality/quantity of work)
- Attitude (positive or negative, willing to help others)

Before you can coach any of your people, you need to observe them performing their important activities. If you manage people involved in customer service functions, for example, watch how they handle customer interactions such as telephone calls,

> **FIVE KEYS TO COACHING SUCCESS**
>
> 1. Observe and Analyze Performance
> 2. Suggest Areas of Improvement
> 3. Model the Desired Method
> 4. Have the Person Try the Desired Method
> 5. Continue Coaching

inquiries, responding to questions, or any other function.

Make it a habit to walk around the office and listen to your people take phone calls and conduct other customer interactions.

When we had a staff to manage, for example, our people knew to expect us. And they knew we would only listen and observe. We didn't jump in or make comments unless they asked for help. It was low key and nonthreatening—and a way to avoid embarrassing the people we coached.

Review projects and interactions. If you manage design engineers, product developers, quality-control technicians, or other types of technical professionals, review their projects on a regular basis. Look at their work habits, planning skills, timeliness, accuracy, quality, and quantity of the work. You should also observe their communication and interpersonal skills when participating in department meetings, co-worker discussions, and customer interactions.

If you're in sales or support, you'll need to observe your people when they interact with customers, clients, and others internally. Customer and client interactions include sales meetings, customer interviews, letter writing, proposals and presentations, project reviews, service appointments, and other important customer-related activities. Internal activities may be department meetings, account reviews, presentations, and even training sessions.

If you are responsible for accounting, administrative, marketing, operational, distribution, or other staff-type functions, you'll again need to observe your people doing their jobs. This also includes their interpersonal communications at meetings, how they prepare and interact at meetings, and project reviews. Observe the quality and timeliness of their work, and any other functions that are important to their performance.

Observe officially. We believe it a smart practice to observe your people officially and unofficially. "Officially" means you tell them in advance you're going to accompany them occasionally to a meeting or an appointment to see them in action. This should be one of the expectations you establish early on so there are no surprises when you ask to tag along with them.

"Unofficially" means observing them casually as you walk by their work area. Stop for a minute or two and just watch them doing their job.

We know an excellent sales manager for one of our clients who would wait at the front door of the office until one of his salespeople was going out of the office for the day. The sales manager would then inform the sales rep that he was riding with the him or her that day. This style may not be right for all managers, but it worked for him.

During these observation sessions, allow people to go about their activities as though you were not there. This can be a little awkward because an employee may want you to conduct the meeting since you're the supervisor or manager.

If a customer is involved, there may be a tendency for the customer to want to deal with you, rather than the regular sales, service, or support representative. Unless you feel it important to handle an item, we suggest the following: When the customer directs the a question to you that your person should respond to, gently direct the customer's question to your representative. ("I'm sure Jim can answer that question better than I can.") The customer will soon understand that you want to keep the other person involved in the account instead of you.

You may even want to have a signal with your people to indicate when you are supposed to handle something or speak on a particular subject. The best customer meetings are always well planned, with each person knowing their role. As the senior manager in such situations, I always tried to stay with the planned agenda and not say anything that might confuse the customer or contradict our people. I didn't want to handle the account, and neither should you. Don't undermine the authority of your people unless you want to manage the account.

Observe unofficially. There are times when you should observe your people in an unofficial capacity. We don't mean spying or eavesdropping on them. We simply mean to casually observe them doing their jobs.

Sometimes people can be very uncomfortable when they know you are observing them. In these situations, just sit and unobtrusively watch, for instance, how a person greets a customer who walks within your earshot. Or pay close attention when one of your people is interacting with a fellow employee.

> ## Best Tip
>
> Observe people 'unofficially' by casually watching them do their jobs, interacting with others, or participating in meetings.

These types of casual conversations can tell you much about the person's interpersonal communication abilities and attitude.

Watching people in action is a great method of collecting data that affects their performance. In some situations it may be the only way to find out where you need to coach them. It also allows you the opportunity to observe them doing good things.

We remember a talented woman responsible for the sales support and forecasting process for an entire personal computer division. She was smart, motivated, and willing to learn. She could quickly analyze the cause of some of the problems we were experiencing with our distribution system and usually knew what to do to fix them.

However, most of the people she worked with were not nearly as quick. This meant that instead of delegating certain tasks for them to do and then following up, she'd do things herself. She thought it was faster. And while it probably was faster, she wasn't helping her people by doing their work. She needed to help them develop skills by coaching them to perform their assignments. Until that happened, she would not be ready for greater responsibility, one of her important goals.

Coaching this person was easy because she wanted to learn how to be more effective. We met regularly for ten to twenty minutes after each forecast meeting to review her performance during the meeting and to see how she was doing with the development of her people.

Best Tip

To help others improve, first ask their opinion of the situation—e.g., 'What could you do differently to get the sale next time?'

This was an opportunity for me to tell her the things she was doing well and give some advice where necessary.

In a few years she ascended to the position of vice president. She earned this promotion, as she had all the others, with her performance.

It is very satisfying to coach talented individuals and see them develop. It's been our privilege to work with many talented people over the years. Coaching them was the best part of each day and mostly responsible for us wanting to start our training-and-development business.

2. Suggest Areas of Improvement

We believe you get better results when you follow a logical, five-step process for helping people improve. The examples that follow are drawn from our experiences helping sales and support people become more productive. Adapt the questions to your situation. You'll find they will work just as well for you as they have for us.

Step One: Ask for the person's opinion. Examples:

1. "What do you think went well at the meeting with the client?"

2. "What do you think the client's priorities are at this time?"

3. "What could you do differently next time?"

Step Two: Provide a sincere compliment. Examples:

1. "You did a nice job developing trust and rapport with the client."

2. "You seemed very comfortable interacting with higher-level executives at the project review session."

3. "You understand the client's internal organization structure."

Step Three: Recommend areas of improvement (limit these to one or two). Examples:

1. "Good questions are so important. Don't you think a few more open-ended questions before talking about our implementation procedures would give you a better understanding of the client's needs?"

2. "Project status reports need to be accurate and timely. If you worked on them immediately after the client review, you'd probably be able to include more details."

3. "We have many talented technical people. Don't get so frustrated. Ask for their help when you need it."

Step Four: Explain the reasons a change will help. Examples:

1. "Open-ended questions allow the client to do most of the talking. That way you can listen for problem areas, goals, and needs. When you do most of the talking, you won't uncover their goals and needs. This makes the implementation of a project more difficult."

2. "You seem to get more of your work done in the morning than in the afternoon. Working on project status reports the next morning at the latest should help you be more accurate."

3. "It is good you want to resolve technical issues on your own. Sometimes though, it is better to ask if people have seen this problem before. Then we service the client better."

Step Five: Ask the person to recommend a better way (Socratic questions). Examples:

1. "How else can you uncover needs and priorities? Is there another way?"

2. "What ideas do you have for completing the project on time?"

COACHING TIPS

1. Coach all the people on your team—the top performers, those in the middle, and those at the bottom.

2. Coach each person one-on-one at least twice a month—and more often when possible. Some people will need more frequent coaching, depending on their development level.

3. Coach your people all the time—even when performance is good.

4. Do not ignore problems and hope they'll get better by themselves. Usually they will not.

5. Avoid jumping in at the first sign of trouble. Don't let people drown, either.

6. Find something positive to say in every coaching session.

7. Have people analyze their performances first. Ask what they like best and least.

8. Recommend and model a preferred method. Team the less-experienced with your best people.

9. Ask for their opinion of the method you've recommended and/or modeled. Give them specific feedback on performance.

10. Practice, practice, practice—in meetings, one-on-one sessions, and role plays.

3. "Where else can you get technical questions answered?"

I (Jack) once managed a technical support manager who came up through the ranks. But I overheard him make a comment one day that showed he forgot that, as a manager, he needed to demonstrate leadership qualities in front of his people instead of trying to remain one of the boys.

Here's what happened. One day I walked into the coffee room where my service manager and a few of his technicians were talking. As I walked in, one of the technicians said, "I really hate working on the system for Mrs. Rendell. She's a real witch when she's having a bad day. And she is always having a bad day."

Then the service manager replied, "I never liked the old lady either when I serviced her account. I think she gets her kicks by pulling the wings off of insects. Just avoid her." They all laughed until they spotted me and the conversation stopped. I said hello to the group and asked the service manager to stop by my office later in the day to discuss the status of a project.

When we met later, I told him what I'd overheard and that it sent a negative message to his people. I asked for his opinion. He agreed it was an inappropriate comment.

Following the coaching process described in the past few pages, I first complimented him for his open relationship with his people. "Your people seem very comfortable to talk about their difficult customer situations," I said. "That's good."

Then I said, "What a great opportunity to coach them on how to deal with difficult people. You know from your experience that dealing with difficult people is part of the job. How would you respond next time?"

For the next ten minutes we discussed some other responses that would allow a positive coaching lesson for his service technicians instead of a negative and unnecessary comment about the customer.

We agreed a better approach would be for the service manager to say something like, "Yes, I remember Mrs. Rendell. She can be difficult. When I was servicing her systems, I learned the best thing to do was to tell her I was there to make things better. I'm part of the solution, not part of the problem."

3. Show (Model) the Desired Method

There are several ways to show your people a desired or preferred method of doing an activity or handling a situation:

A. In a private meeting

- Talk over the desired method first
- Give an example

- Demonstrate or explain the desired method
- Discuss what is different
- Ask for their reaction

Talk over the situation, and give an example of the behavior that needs to be addressed. You may want to demonstrate or explain the desired method you'd like the person to follow. Discuss what is different about the new approach, and then ask for a reaction and opinion. Talk over the desired approach, give an example or two of how you think something should be said or done. Discuss what is different about the desired method and ask for a reaction.

B. In a team meeting

- Talk over the desired method first
- Give some examples
- Demonstrate or explain the desired method to the team
- Discuss what is different
- Debrief—ask for their reactions

When more than one of your people need help with a problem, a team meeting can be an effective and efficient way of coaching. As with the one-on-one meeting, describe the situation with the team or group and explain the behavior that needs to be addressed. Demonstrate or explain the desired method you'd like people to follow. (You can demonstrate, or you can have a team member do it.) As a group, discuss what is different about the new approach and then ask for your team's reaction and opinion.

Here is an idea for your next team meeting: Try delegating this portion of a meeting to a promising individual on your team. We've found it is a great way to help develop their coaching skills and ready them for additional responsibility. It can also be a lot of fun, and it's a great team-building activity.

C. Role playing ("curb-side" coaching)

- Talk over the desired method first

- Let the person play the role of the client, customer, or what have you
- You play the role of the person being coached
- Role play the situation
- Demonstrate the improved skill
- Debrief the role play for feedback

With interpersonal skills coaching, you can have your people see the desired method in a safe environment by role playing or with a practice exercise. Role playing can be done either one-on-one or at team meetings. One-on-one meetings are often referred to as "curb-side coaching" because such sessions have been known to occur outside a client's office just before or just after a meeting.

The manager can model the desired method for the individual or for the entire team. As the manager and coach, you should play the role of your team member and let him or her be the other person. This allows you to demonstrate the desired method. This is an effective way for people to practice the important skills that will make them more effective.

Best Tip

Don't ignore performance problems in the hope that they'll get better over time. They won't.

D. Actual client or customer meeting (curb-side coaching)

- Talk over the desired method first.
- Plan the meeting. The manager takes the lead in front of the client.
- Analyze what was good or bad immediately upon completion.

If you work with sales or support people, you may want to demonstrate a desired method for a customer interaction when in front of the customer or client. This real-time training process allows your people to see you in action. Talk over what you will do in front of the customer in advance. Plan the steps you will follow and, after your meeting, analyze what was done. Having your people watch you do something is a great form of coaching that serves as a teaching experience and enhances your personal credibility.

4. Have the Person Try the Desired Method

Again, you have several methods to choose from:

A. In a private meeting

- Talk over the desired method first
- Have the person try the desired method
- Observe and analyze performance
- Ask for his or her opinion
- Provide specific feedback
- Gain commitment to practice and continue the desired method

B. In a team meeting

- Talk over the desired method first
- Have the person try the desired method in a group
- Observe and analyze performance
- Debrief—ask for a reaction
- Provide specific feedback
- Gain commitment to practice and continue the desired method

C. Role playing (curb-side coaching)

- Talk over the desired method first
- The manager plays the client (or whoever)
- Role play the client situation or last meeting
- Encourage the person to "customize" the method
- Debrief the role play

D. Actual client meeting (curb-side coaching)

- Talk over the desired method first
- Plan the meeting
- Analyze the meeting immediately upon leaving

You need to have people try the desired approach or method. Provide feedback, coaching comments, or tips. Once again, you can select a one-on-one "curb-side" coaching session or team meeting.

Role playing is one of the best methods we know of to help your people practice, especially for soft skills, because it is done in a "safe" environment (team meeting or one-on-one). Some people love to role play and others will liken it to playing poker for pretzels because it isn't for real. But it is practice, and we believe people do not perform any better than they practice.

Role playing is especially good for coaching your new or less-experienced people. It is also good for coaching experienced people to do new things.

5. *Continue Coaching*

In short:

- Repeat the process until people have mastered the method
- Compliment positive performance
- Recommend enhancements
- Encourage them to study or practice

Step five is to continue coaching until the individual has mastered the desired method. Depending on what you're coaching, this could take some time. Be patient and allow people the latitude to learn by "internalizing" the approach you're recommending in a way that suits their ability and skill level. You don't want to create robots, so allow them to adapt the method as long as it accomplishes the results needed. Be sure to compliment positive performances and recommend enhancements.

Further, encourage people to study or practice more on their own. And encourage them to seek your help when necessary. People will often recognize their shortcomings and needed areas of improvement. Create an atmosphere in which your people are comfortable asking you for help.

Finally, remember that Rome wasn't built in a day. Developing new ways to do activities will take time. Practice doesn't make perfect. Perfect practice makes perfect. We have noticed, during our development seminars, that the most experienced people will often learn something the fastest because they know what to do with a new idea or technique. These people are professionals who understand they are never too old to learn something new if it can help them in their jobs.

A good example of this is what happens at any professional golf tournament. If you get the opportunity to go, watch these talented professionals practice specific elements of their game before and after they complete a round. What makes people professional is the hours of practice they put into improving their skills. Most of their practice is never seen by the average person. Practice and hard work are important elements that help talented people succeed.

Work with Your Senior People

It is tempting for a manager to assume that senior people already have excellent skills. Even the most experienced people in any line of work can experience problems from time to time. When these problems go unchecked, they can become habits, bad habits. If you observe them just as you observe your other people, you'll know what they do well and where they may need some coaching. You must think hard about the particular person and the particular job they need to do. The coaching you do will vary depending on the situation and the development levels of your people.

Many managers feel that working with senior people is more interesting and rewarding. Others prefer to work with less-experienced people. The real world requires that you coach all levels. Each situation is different and the manager must adjust his or her coaching to be effective. What works in one situation may not work in another.

Our experience is this: Coaching your senior people involves the same basic steps as coaching others on your team.

Coaching By The Numbers

What To Do	*When To Do It*	*How To Do It*
1. Observe and Analyze Performance	At least once a month (More often is better)	✔ Watch them work; travel with them ✔ Pinpoint their strengths and weaknesses
2. Suggest Areas of Improvement	Immediately	✔ Ask what activities they do well, not so well ✔ Compliment them ✔ Ask what they could do to improve performance ✔ Make recommendations ✔ Give examples
3. Show the Desired Method	ASAP/before the day is over	✔ Role play alone or at next meeting ✔ One-on-one session ✔ Mini-training session ✔ Team meeting ✔ Role play exercises ✔ Formal training
4. Have the Person Try the Desired Method	ASAP/before the day is over Next meeting	✔ Role play alone or at next meeting ✔ Mini-training session/role play
5. Continue Coaching	Ongoing	✔ Repeat process

The big difference is how you deliver the message and accomplish the objective—correcting a problem. You don't want to embarrass a person who has dedicated most of his or her adult life to a company, profession, or career. You do want to correct a problem that you see and get the person to change an approach or actions.

Have faith in the experience of your senior people and ask them to think of other situations where they did things differently. This lets them know you've recognized a problem area and want to help. But it allows them to figure it out for themselves based on their experience.

If a situation comes up where they don't have experience in an area, you as the manager must recommend a better way. Just because someone has many years of practice doing something doesn't mean they know everything. How you get to the solution is the key.

And don't worry if you're younger than the person you're coaching. We have seen many situations where a young manager coaches older people. Age is not the issue. What matters most is recognizing a problem area, communicating it effectively to the individual (whether senior or junior), and developing or recommending a viable solution.

The first item on the Agile Manager's agenda when he arrived at the office was an account review session with Jeff Lewis, one of his senior account managers. Jeff was a seasoned veteran who grew up and attended college in the metropolitan New York City area. The review was to discuss the results of a customer meeting held the week before in Austin, Texas.

The Agile Manager received a phone call late Friday afternoon from Peter Thompson, the customer, saying he was concerned about the business relationship between the two companies. Thompson said these concerns finally came to a head during a meeting with Jeff earlier that day.

Thompson told the Agile Manager that Jeff's "account management style" was the problem. The meeting earlier that day was the latest example of their problem with Jeff.

Thompson said, "Jeff works too fast, which creates careless mistakes. He leaves a trail of dead bodies—open issues—behind him. We can't clean up after him any more. These mistakes have resulted in a delay of an important project we're working on."

The Agile Manager knew it also resulted in a loss of faith in

Jeff's ability to handle the account effectively. Peter Thompson asked the Agile Manager for a new account manager to handle their relationship or they would "take their business elsewhere."

Any time a customer called with a complaint about an account manager, it was a serious problem. Compounding this situation was the fact that Jeff was a seasoned performer with a good track record. Obviously there was a personality clash, which the Agile Manager knew happens from time to time. But this was more serious, and the Agile Manager wanted to hear Jeff's side of the story.

Jeff uses a fast-paced, New York style in business. This had always been an asset for Jeff. The Agile Manager had been to at least twenty customer meetings with Jeff, and his style had never been a problem.

The Agile Manager felt there was no alternative but to grant Peter Thompson's request and change account managers. Jeff's ego could handle that. What concerned the Agile Manager even more was what to do about Jeff's style. A one-on-one coaching session was in order to make sure Jeff could be effective with customers in Texas or any other location outside of New York.

"Hello, Jeff. Did you have a good weekend?" asked the Agile Manager, peering into Jeff's office.

"Great! I played golf Saturday and shot my best game of the year," said Jeff. "How about you?"

"We had the family over for a cookout," said the Agile Manager. "It's a great time of year. Let's take a walk to the cafeteria. I could use a cup of coffee. Tell me about your meeting last week in Texas."

"It wasn't bad," replied Jeff. "I met with Peter Thompson and the project committee for about an hour. We were supposed to meet for two hours, but something else came up. Thompson said he would have to cut the meeting short by one hour. I was still able to cover the important items I had."

"Jeff, that's not what I heard," said the Agile Manager. "I got a call from Peter Thompson on Friday. He said they were unhappy with your management style. He said you operate too fast for them and you make careless mistakes. They want me to take you off their account or they won't do business with us."

"What? They didn't say anything about this to me," Jeff shot back immediately. " What did I do?"

"I'm not exactly sure," said the Agile Manager. "Peter Thompson said your conduct during the meeting last week was the latest example of your carelessness. It sounds like you pushed them over the edge when you tried to cover too much in a one-hour meeting."

"Well they didn't ask many questions," said Jeff. "Thompson said he'd get back to me in a week or so. I planned on following up this week."

The Agile Manager continued, "Thompson also said you've left a trail of open issues or what he called 'dead bodies' behind and they were tired of cleaning up after you. Jeff, I think you dropped the ball on some things you were supposed to do for them. Thompson said that caused an important project to be delayed and they've had enough. They want someone else handling their account."

"I just don't understand," said Jeff. "My other customers don't have these kind of issues with me. What is it with these guys?"

The Agile Manager said, "Jeff, think about this situation for a minute. What are you doing that would cause them to feel so uncomfortable about you?"

"I guess it's because I'm from New York and they're from Texas. My style must be too fast for them," said Jeff.

"I don't think that's it," said the Agile Manager. "You're much too experienced not to read and adapt to different personality styles. I think it's the details you're not following up on that's caused the problem."

"I'm getting tired of doing all the detail work," said Jeff. "I'm one of the most senior people here. They could do some of the detail work themselves or I should have more help. Why should I still be the person watching the details? I'm capable of a lot more than that."

Aha, thought the Agile Manager, catching a whiff of the real problem. Lack of attention to details, while the source of the problem with Thompson, is a symptom of a deeper problem. Let me play a hunch and see if I can smoke out the real reason, then coach and counsel him.

"Tell me Jeff, why did you really turn down the promotion of the district manager position we talked about last year?" asked the Agile Manager. "You said you were happy in this area and didn't want to relocate. Was that the real reason?"

"That was part of it," responded Jeff. "I would have taken the job and moved my family if it were a promotion to vice president. But it was one full level below your position, and I didn't want to move for that title."

"You could have developed that job into VP level with a good year or two," said the Agile Manager. "You know people get promoted to vice president for the results they accomplish."

"I guess I feel I've already earned it," replied Jeff.

"Not according to Peter Thompson and how you managed their account," said the Agile Manager. "But I think this is an isolated case. You know what it takes to manage relationships at an account. I think your attitude affected your judgment and your actions. We both know you can manage the details and can adapt to the different personality styles of your customers. It's what helped you to be successful for so many years."

"I guess I really screwed up the Thompson situation, didn't I?" asked Jeff.

"We've got some work to do. Shall I call him and see if we can meet again this week and straighten out this situation together? I'd like to try to keep you managing the account." replied the Agile Manager. "But the final decision is up to Peter Thompson."

"Please call him and see what you can do," said Jeff. "I'd hate to lose an account this way. I'm better than that."

"Yes you are, Jeff," said the Agile Manager. "I'll call him as soon as I get back to my office. Let's get this customer happy again and then we can look to the future. You've still got a bright future ahead of you. I know you can earn the vice president position you want."

The Agile Manager felt that the most rewarding part of having leadership responsibility was seeing the positive impact of his coaching and counseling. As his career developed and he progressed through the ranks of middle management into senior executive positions, he felt fortunate having helped many of his people make that same progression over the years.

He especially liked counseling to help people develop their careers. He himself had been fortunate to have a good friend and business associate take him under his wing many years ago. Among the many great pieces of advice he received during those counseling sessions, one in particular made a very big impression. That message was to "develop your people through solid coaching and counseling sessions so that there is always at least one person on your team ready to take over your responsibilities."

The Agile Manager knew that approach had not only helped him in his own career advancement, but it also had a direct impact on the lives of the people that he was grooming. He knew he had made a difference in many lives and felt confident that those same people would do the same in the future for other members of their own teams.

The Agile Manager's Checklist

✔ Observe and analyze performance continually. It's the foundation for effective coaching.

✔ Ask the people you coach for their opinions on how things are going and how they could do better.

✔ Whenever you can—at customer sites, in the office, over the phone, at meetings—*show* people how you want them to act or behave.

✔ Continue coaching until the person masters the method. Then start in on the next lesson.

✔ When coaching senior people, follow the same steps you would with a rookie. But take care not to embarrass them.

Chapter Seven

Confront Constructively

*"Failure to confront is just like giving permission
to continue behaving poorly."*

JACK CULLEN AND LEN D'INNOCENZO

The Agile Manager hung up the telephone, upset. One of the division's top customers just cancelled a $400,000 order for personal computers scheduled for delivery the following month. The customer cited "poor communication" and "unresponsiveness" as the reasons for canceling the order. This customer needed to upgrade the disk drives on thirty older personal computer systems used within his business and was tired of waiting for the spare disk-drive kits.

The customer, frustrated about the lack of action on the disk-drive kits, canceled the order for new computers to show his dissatisfaction.

During the phone conversation, the Agile Manager checked the inventory list and explained to the customer that these particular kits were in high demand, and listed as on backorder with no delivery date noted. But the customer said he had heard this all before. He had tried—without luck—to get a straight answer on two previous occasions to determine when the upgrade kits would be delivered. "They've been backordered for over three months," shouted the customer. "We can't wait any longer. We've got a business to run. Your people don't know what they're doing."

The Agile Manager tried, unsuccessfully, to calm down the irate customer.

The inventory system and the people involved with this important customer failed. Critical delivery information was not available, and the customer believed that nobody in the Agile Manager's organization cared.

What upset the Agile Manager the most was the timing. It was too late to save the new-computer order, and even more importantly, this important customer. The Agile Manager remembered—painfully—an article he read in *Fortune Magazine* in January of 1998. It stated that it is ten times more expensive to win new customers than to keep existing ones—*ten times* more expensive. The entire situation could have been avoided.

The Agile Manager knew something had to be done to avoid any similar problems. Keeping customers satisfied with high-quality products and service was the top priority.

His next telephone call was to Michael Roberts, the salesperson assigned to cover the account. Michael was a veteran performer and reported to Derek Mayfield, the Midwest regional manager. Michael said he was expecting the phone call from the Agile Manager. He had suggested the customer call the Agile Manager directly to cancel the order. Michael was just as frustrated as the customer. He opened the account originally and would have to make up the lost sales revenue with his other accounts.

"Michael, when did you know the customer might cancel the order?" asked the Agile Manager.

"Last week," replied Michael. "I told Derek and he said he would look into the delivery status of the kits that were on backorder."

"Did Derek get back to you with an answer?" asked the Agile Manager.

"Yes, but he couldn't get an answer from the inventory manager as to when the kits could be delivered. He was going to kick the problem up to you. That's why I asked the customer to call you. I was hoping you had the delivery information and could save the order for me."

"I'm sorry I didn't have the information. I was not aware of the problem with the backordered kits. I promise you I'll look into it and get you an answer," said the Agile Manager.

The Agile Manager's next call was to Derek Mayfield, Michael's manager. He explained the events of the day and asked for Derek's side of the story.

"I couldn't get a straight answer from anyone in the inventory department regarding the kits," said Derek. "I called several times and couldn't get anyone that knew what was going on. They are really screwed up in that department."

"That may be true," said the Agile Manager. "I just wish you asked me to get involved with this problem when you couldn't get an answer. Now we've lost an order for $400,000 and a key account."

"You're not blaming me for the customer canceling the order are you?" asked Derek. "It wasn't my fault!"

"I'm not blaming anyone," said the Agile Manager. "I need to research what is going on with these kits. I'm scheduled to be in your office next week, Derek," said the Agile Manager. "Let's meet for breakfast. I'll research the kit situation and we can review what happened and what we should do in the future."

Confrontations with subordinate employees and peers are part of a manager's responsibility. How you approach each confrontation can determine your effectiveness and success. It would be wonderful if the need to confront your people or others you work with were only a once-in-a-while affair. However, things usually don't work out this way. Whenever someone demonstrates unproductive performance, or inappropriate behavior, you as the manager have an obligation to confront.

Confront negative behavior as soon as it is apparent. If you don't, the behavior will worsen, causing more problems down the road. Confronting early can give you an opportunity to coach constructively rather than discipline.

Confrontations can be destructive or constructive. Constructive confrontation minimizes a person's defensive reactions and sets the stage for productive coaching to begin. Even when the manager has to take action fast, the process can be positive rather than negative. We'll show you how to confront constructively and positively.

Keep Three Techniques for Managing Conflict in Your Toolbox

There are three primary methods for managing conflicts with and among your subordinates. Each has a place in your management tool box. Selecting the proper tool for managing conflicts will depend on the situation. The three are:

1. The Benevolent Dictator Approach. In this technique, the manager directs (orders) his or her subordinates to follow specific instructions without question. There is no discussion and the penalty for failing to follow the manager's directives is severe, up to and including termination.

| Best Tip

Use the 'dictator' style of managing only when you're dealing with policies, laws, or mandated procedures.

We suggest you use this approach only when you need to have company policies followed with no questions asked. Policies might include the safekeeping of company property, or handling cash and other valuable assets. You also need to use the dictator approach when it comes to having employees adhere to all applicable laws.

There is no other acceptable method of dealing with these types of situations other than for employees to follow company policy, or society's laws, to the letter.

2. The Socratic Questioning Approach. This technique allows you to manage a conflict by questioning the people involved. You use questions to uncover the source of the conflict and allow employees to come up with solutions on their own. This assumes a high level of maturity and a willingness to want to resolve the problem.

This approach works best with the managers and supervisors who report to you and other senior-level or experienced people. The questions you ask are intended to get the individuals to reflect on the situation and decide for themselves an alternative approach. Using this method with managers, supervisors, and other senior-level people gives them a chance to rethink what was done and determine a better way on their own.

Here are some examples of Socratic questions:

- What problems arise when you get frustrated and make negative comments in front of your people?
- What message do you send to your people when they see you act negatively?
- What could you do differently next time to avoid getting so frustrated?
- What advantages will come from you being more positive?
- How can you make sure you stay positive in front of your people?

3. The "Constructive Confrontation" Approach. The constructive confrontation technique allows the manager and subordinate to analyze a conflict situation and develop possible solutions together. It is constructive in nature and attempts to preserve the dignity and ego of the subordinate. It deals with the problem instead of descending into a personal attack on an individual. Caring confrontations tend to be more constructive because you are also coaching the individual to overcome a problem or to learn a specific technique.

Create the Right Conditions to Confront

If you want to coach and confront your people constructively, create the right emotional environment and conditions for the process to work effectively.

Here are some things to keep in mind that will help you create the right conditions:

1. Strive to keep the conversation businesslike and without

emotion, to preserve the employee's self-esteem.

2. When it's possible, have your meeting at a neutral site (conference room, cafeteria, restaurant, etc.).

3. Make the confrontation one-on-one.

4. Keep your relationship professional.

5. Separate the facts from the fiction.

6. Be positive and constructive, not judgmental.

7. Avoid indirect or ambiguous statements, speak plainly.

8. Avoid making a speech or giving a lecture.

9. Confront behavior, not motives.

10. Focus on the problem at hand, not incidents from the past.

11. Suggest or request specific actions rather than demand.

12. Maintain your composure and stay cool and professional.

Use the Constructive Confrontation Process

We prefer the "Constructive Confrontation" approach for conflict management whenever possible. It has several advantages over the other techniques discussed. It allows you to be relevant as the manager, confronting the problem rather than personalities. You also avoid long lecture sessions or speeches. Constructive confrontation tends to be more interactive because there are fewer accusations.

1. Analyze the Situation. The first step of the constructive confrontation process is to gather the facts. You need to determine what actually happened. What caused the problem? What were the circumstances? Who was involved? What was said? Was there a misunderstanding or lack of communication? What were the consequences of the inappropriate behavior?

Avoid jumping to conclusions or making assumptions too fast. As a coach and manager, it is important that you understand as many of the details as you can before the actual confrontation. If you are dealing with a reoccurring problem, review your notes or think about the last confrontation or coaching session you had with your employee.

You definitely want to avoid a common mistake we've seen

all too often. Over the years that we have been training and developing managers to be coaches, we've seen too many people conduct the confrontation with only part of the story. They get only a portion of the facts or, worse yet, they get incorrect information.

This creates a huge problem for the manager during the confrontation. Now time is spent sorting out the facts instead of coaching and confronting people constructively. The manager loses credibility, and emotions can run high.

Be smart and research the facts before conducting the confrontation. This shows you did your homework and prepared professionally. If you must confront your people because of a situation, take the time and gather the right information and analyze the situation in advance. Proper prior planning will prevent poor performance by the manager and coach.

Best Tip

Before you confront, make sure you have the facts right. If you don't, it'll blow your case and you'll lose credibility.

2. Set Up a Meeting. We suggest you schedule a meeting rather than make a telephone call or have a casual hallway conversation. If the confrontation is to be effective, make it a formal meeting. A neutral site such as a conference room, restaurant, or the quiet corner of the company cafeteria or coffee room will do.

Set up the meeting with a phone call or e-mail. Mention the topic to be discussed. Let the person know the matter is important. Avoid surprising her. Tell her if she needs to prepare any information or bring along any items. Give her a chance to prepare properly.

3. Build Rapport. Once you have selected a neutral setting that is quiet and free of interruption, earn the right to confront the negative behavior by showing a sincere interest in the employee as a person. Build rapport by making a sincere compliment, or recalling a recent event that was positive. This gets the meeting off to a cordial start and may help to remove some of the nervous anticipation the employee is probably feeling.

Keep in mind you want to confront the negative behavior, not alienate the individual. Show you genuinely care about him or her as a person before you present the problem. This will set the stage for a more productive session.

Best Tip
When confronting, explain the facts of the situation, then show how the behavior resulted in a problem.

Once when confronting an employee about being late for a number of scheduled meetings, we talked about the young man's children and their interest in soccer. This was pleasant for him to discuss since he was at a soccer game over the weekend and his child had scored a goal.

It also served as a perfect transition into the man's tardiness problem, since a soccer team depends on its members to show up on time for practices and games. The man's problem stemmed more from a lack of planning than a bad attitude. The discussion about the man's child and the soccer team was an effective example. For the next four years this man was on the staff, he was never late for a meeting again. The confrontation was caring, and effective.

4. Present the Problem. After you build rapport, say that you have a problem. Don't say "we have a problem," unless you share responsibility. If the problem is the result of the employee's negative action or unproductive behavior, look him or her in the eyes and say, directly, "You have a problem."

Explain the facts of the situation as you understand them, without embellishment. Explain the results of the behavior. To avoid making the person overly defensive, be as nonjudgmental as possible.

You also don't want the employee to minimize the problem, so show her you've done your homework. Explain the people you've spoken with, the facts you've gathered, why the negative behavior is unacceptable, and the consequences of the behavior.

Remain as unemotional as possible (this may be difficult), and discuss what happened as a result of the negative action or unproductive behavior. Don't speculate on the motives or reasons for the behavior. Just state the facts.

5. Ask Clarifying and Exploratory Questions. Next, ask open-ended clarifying questions and exploratory probes. Let her tell her side of the story.

You may want to prepare a few of these questions in advance. Saying "Please explain what happened," is much better that asking, "Why would you do that?" Some other good questions you may want to use include:

"What were you trying to do?"

"What did you think would happen?"

"What made you select that course of action?"

"What were you hoping to accomplish?"

Listen actively to her responses, focus on what she says and how she says it. Send her the right signals with your body language. Look directly at her. If the situation is complicated, you may want to take a few notes so you don't miss anything. This will also help you to keep the facts straight in the event you want to document your meeting.

Most importantly, be sure you both agree on the cause of the problem behavior and the effect of the actions. This is a critical step in the caring confrontation process. Discussing possible solutions with the employee will be meaningless unless she acknowledges the problem.

6. Discuss Possible Solutions. Now comes the fun part for most coaches—discussing possible solutions to correct the negative or unproductive behavior. This is where coaches earn their pay and, we believe, get their greatest satisfaction.

Until you discuss possible solutions with the employee you are only a manager. When you discuss possible solutions to correct the problem behavior, you're coaching.

If the problem is the employee's, does she accept responsibil-

PRESENT THE PROBLEM PROPERLY

There's an art to confronting an employee in a caring manner. Take these steps, and you should do fine:

1. Take Ownership. Indicate that this is not just the employee's problem, if you share responsibility. It is yours, too, until it is resolved. Let him know you are going to stay involved—that you will see it through to completion.

Make an opening statement like:

- "Phil, we have to talk about a problem that affects both of us."

If you do not share responsibility, say something like:

- "Steve, you have a problem and we need to talk about it."

2. Describe Your Feelings. Think how you really feel about the situation and tell the employee. It is important for him to know your honest feelings, so tell him. Do you feel disappointed, unhappy, upset, disturbed, worried, puzzled, angry, frustrated, concerned?

Some examples might be:

- "I am worried about your sales performance for the last two months."
- "I am very concerned about the accuracy of your work."

3. Describe the Behavior. What is bothering you? What has you upset or concerned? What did the employee do or fail to do that has caused the problem? What actions or activities were not satisfactory? Examples:

- "You are running well behind schedule on two highly visible projects."

- "You are rushing to finish each project and not checking your work.

4. State the Facts. Talk about what actually happened—what was observed and verified. Show you did your research and state the facts clearly. Avoid any embellishments, assumptions, or interpretations. Some examples:

- "The status report shows that each project is only 50 percent complete."
- "You're spending too much time on personal telephone calls."

5. State the Effect. Say what could happen if the negative behavior continues. Examples:

- "This level of performance is not acceptable. You will not finish any of these projects on time, and that could mean financial penalties to our company."
- "This hurts our entire department and reflects badly on your performance. You will never get the promotion you want with this level of performance."

ity? What can you as the manager and coach do to help? Should you get involved, and if so, what should you do? Gain agreement on who will do what and by when. Be clear on the steps that will be followed and who is responsible for what actions.

Some situations will call for you to use a Socratic method of coaching. This method, best used with experienced people, is where you ask the employee for his or her opinion to a problem. Good questions include, "What would you do differently next time?" Or, "If you were coaching someone, what would you suggest he do?"

Be careful when asking questions that look for solutions to problem behavior with less-experienced people. It can actually be counterproductive. Asking people for a solution when they are new or inexperienced in a job can frustrate them, and you will end up losing credibility as a coach.

A few years back, we recommended the son of a friend of ours for a position with one of our clients. He had just graduated from college and was hired as a junior sales representative. As with most people new to sales, this young man needed the guidance and experience of a good manager and coach. Unfortunately, what he received was lots of management but not much coaching.

Once, when the young rep's territory was being reviewed, the manager determined that there were no strong relationships with upper level executives. Instead of offering to help the young rep develop these relationships, the manager simply said, "You need to develop your relationships with the executives at your top accounts. How will you go about doing this? What can you do to strengthen these relationships?"

Best Tip

Always discuss possible solutions to performance problems with the employee. That makes you a coach and not a mere manager.

The young rep was frustrated because he didn't know "how" to do what his manager was asking. He was inexperienced, new to the industry, and very uncomfortable interacting with people twice his age. In retrospect, we believe this particular manager didn't know how to develop executive-level relationships himself. Instead of coaching the sales rep and leading by example, he made the young man feel uncomfortable and frustrated.

7. Follow-Up and Inspire. It is very important to follow up with the employee and monitor progress and results. You also want to inspire your people by letting them know you are interested in their progress. Let them know you're interested in how they're doing and what else you can do as their coach to help. You want to focus on the positives and provide encouragement whenever you can.

This may sound like we're suggesting you act as a cheerleader—

and we are! People want to hear encouragement from their manager and coach. Coaching is not a once-in-a-while activity. It is ongoing. Following up with your people on specific coaching you've done will earn you right to continue coaching.

The Agile Manager next walked over to the inventory department to speak with Pete Stancowski, the manager. Stancowski was a twenty-plus-years employee with a good reputation. The Agile Manager appraised Pete of the situation with the backordered kits and the canceled customer order.

Pete looked up the status of the kits on his computer terminal and said "Yup, they're backordered all right. We must have a problem getting the disk drives from our supplier. I see there are another two hundred kits on backorder besides the thirty your customer is looking for."

The Agile Manager responded, "Pete, he's not our customer anymore. He canceled the kit order plus another order for $400,000 worth of new PC systems. Why are the kits backordered?"

"I don't know," said Pete. "Let me ask Mary Lou. She's responsible for all the kit inventory."

They walked to Mary Lou's cubicle only to learn that she too had no idea why the disk-drive upgrade kits were on back order. Her records indicated that there was an item missing from the kit parts list. Mary Lou reminded Pete that company policy stated that a kit could not be shipped to a customer if it was missing any parts.

"What parts are missing?" asked the Agile Manager.

"It looks like it's four knurled-knob mounting screws used to secure the disk drive to the computer's chassis. They're what's holding up the kits from shipping. They come from a specialty supplier and the lead time is twenty-eight weeks," responded Mary Lou. "We ordered them ninety days ago."

"Twenty-eight weeks," said Pete. "Why so long for mounting screws?"

"I'll print out the bill of materials and we can take a look," said Mary Lou.

The bill of materials for the kit showed that in addition to the disk drive, the only other items that were part of the kit were the four knurled-knob mounting screws and an instruction sheet for installation. The knurled-knob mounting screws were a special design that allowed a person to install the disk drive without using a screwdriver. The technician could just tighten the mounting screws by turning the knurled knobs with two fingers.

"Does this mean we're backordered for over two hundred disk drive upgrade kits because we can't substitute a mounting screw?" asked Pete Stancowski.

The Agile Manager was doing an excellent job of remaining silent. "That's the company policy," said Mary Lou. "We can't ship an incomplete kit."

Finally the Agile Manager spoke, "That company policy, four mounting screws, and a bad job communicating just cost us a $400,00 order and an important customer."

Mary Lou continued, "Well, you two are really not going to like this. It says here that the four knurled knobs are only extra anyway, in case the technician drops one of the screws that are already in the chassis.

"Wait a minute. That means we lost a $400,000 order because of four screws that weren't needed in the first place!" shouted Pete. "That's just beautiful."

"That's right," said Mary Lou. "Can you believe it?"

The Agile Manager said, "Thank you for the information Mary Lou. Pete I wish you or Mary Lou could have given this information to Derek Mayfield when he called last week. He and Michael Roberts might have been able to save the customer and the order by substituting a few screws."

When they returned to Pete Stancowski's office and the door was closed, Pete said to the Agile Manager, "I'm really sorry. My people didn't do a good job here. The system failed us and my people are all very busy. I'll speak with them about responding to inquiries from the field faster."

"Pete, I know how busy your people are," responded the Agile Manager. "When our salespeople in the field make inquiries regarding customer orders, they need your department's help to get accurate information to their customers quickly. When one of us fails, we all fail. We're all on the same team. We can't be successful unless we all help each other."

He took a deep breath and continued. "I'm happy you'll be speaking with your people about being more responsive. If they can get information for you or me when we ask for it, they should be able to do the same for our field people. I'll be speaking with Derek Mayfield next week about how he could have handled this situation differently. We all could have done a better job with this customer. Hopefully we can avoid a situation like this from happening in the future."

"I promise this won't happen again," said Pete. "I'll call a meeting right away."

"Good. Now I have to send an e-mail to our VP of engineering about changing company policy. We shouldn't hold up shipping a disk drive kit because we're missing parts that aren't needed in the first place. Company policy has to change."

"What will you say?" asked Pete.

"I'll tell the story of how we lost a good customer and an order for $400,000 because we were missing four extra knurled-knob screws and we couldn't get that information to the customer," said the Agile Manager. "I'm going to call it 'The $400,000 screw.'"

"It sounds like a classic," said Pete. "I'd sure like to see that e-mail. Will you please copy me?"

The Agile Manager replied "You'll get a copy—and so will our CEO."

Important: Repetition and Desire

Bringing about a positive behavior change usually requires more than one confrontation and ongoing coaching sessions. In order to change people's behavior, they must first want to change. If they do not have the desire to change something in their life, multiple discussions will probably not work.

The secret to changing behavior is desire on the part of the person—and ongoing coaching and counseling by the manager.

Think about some of the many diet programs that are popular today. Millions of people around the world attend weekly meetings to hear advice on healthy cooking and eating habits. People learn how to prepare tasty foods at home and eat right when away from home regardless of how busy they are.

At these sessions, they also record their weight to track and monitor their weight loss progress. None of this will work unless they attend these weekly sessions and follow the prescribed eating plan the rest of the week. But the combination of the advice they receive (coaching) and the support they hear from the other people in the program (counseling) helps to motivate their desire to be successful.

This approach works with the people you need to coach. A strong desire to succeed (internal motivation) coupled with your sound advice and guidance (coaching) on a regular basis will bring about lasting behavior change.

Read Defenses

Confrontations often cause subordinates or peers to be tense, uncomfortable, and afraid. Their reaction may be to stand and fight or to turn and run. They will often turn their energy into creating a defense, rather than recognizing and working to resolve the conflict.

There are several defensive mechanisms a subordinate or peer might use to diffuse or avoid the confrontation:

1. **Denial of the problem.** Denial of a problem by the employee will greatly limit the effectiveness of any coaching by the manager. If the individual will not admit that there is a problem, he won't have the motivation or desire needed to change. A second problem is when he takes the position that it wasn't his fault, or that you must have him confused with someone else. This is where you as the manager and coach need to do your homework in advance. Be sure of your facts before you confront the individual. This saves time and avoids confusion.

2. **Minimizing the importance of the problem.** Sometimes

the employee will try to minimize the significance of a problem when compared to other events that are going on. This is another defense mechanism people use to attempt to change the issue away from them to something else they think is more important.

A subordinate from a few years ago comes to mind. A very talented marketing manager worked for me (Len), but he was habitually late submitting his weekly expense reports. One or two months would pass and then he would rush in and expect me to sign five or six weeks' worth of expense reports with little or no review. This behavior was quite unacceptable and required a confrontation.

Best Tip

Understand that correcting performance problems usually requires more than just one confrontation.

The individual tried to minimize the problem because of his busy schedule and the lack of enough people in the marketing department to do all the work. It was true. The man was very busy and the marketing department was understaffed by one person. But these were not the real issues.

The real issues were his lack of discipline and poor management habits. These poor habits were symptoms of greater problems that were also hurting his performance. As creative and talented as he was, he would never be promoted unless he could demonstrate personal discipline and control. He also needed to prove he was ready for greater responsibility.

This point was the real consequence of his behavior. He wanted to be promoted and did not want people (especially me) to think he was a poor manager. His motivation was clear, so we discussed the management habits he needed to develop. We also talked about the personal discipline required to focus what was important so that his projects were completed on time. The side benefit to the company was that the marketing department was as creative as before and the marketing manager was now able to coach and develop his people. He was now ready for more responsibility.

3. Diminishing the source of the complaint or its credibility. Another defensive position will be to diminish the source or the credibility of the person making the complaint. Whoever brought the problem up is not important, or the source of the complaint is unreliable. In either case, the employee is just trying to avoid the confrontation. You need to have the facts together to rebuff this type of defense.

4. Diffusion to another person or another issue. This defensive approach can be a problem for some managers, because we do not live in a perfect world. The manager will hear from the subordinate that the complaint is not the real issue, something else is. Or that the employee is not the problem, someone else is.

In the real world, there are always other issues that may be related but are not relevant to the problem with the subordinate. These other issues will run the gamut of everyday business problems to market, industry, and even international problems. Once again, it is simply a defensive mechanism by the subordinate to diffuse the situation away from him or her to something or someone else. As a leader, manager, and coach, you can not allow this situation to occur. If you do, expect to hear this defense again and again.

Best Tip

Get employees to admit a problem exists. If they don't, you'll have a hard time coaching effectively.

5. It's an impossible situation. If the situation seems impossible—beyond the control of the subordinate—there may be a tendency by the employee to say "Nothing can be done, so why bother?"

Think about going to the post office to get additional stamps because the postal rates have just been increased. This situation happened to me, Len, not long ago.

I skipped lunch and waited in a long line at our local post office. After fifteen minutes, I got to the front of the line and encountered a postal clerk who could not care less about my time. He informed me that they were all sold out of the new stamps I waited in line to buy. They were also sold out of one-cent stamps needed to use the old postage stamps in our office. I was frustrated, a little cranky, and I snapped at the postal employee. "How can the post office be out of the new stamps? You announced the increase three months ago! How am I supposed to send out mail?"

The postal employee was equally frustrated, having heard the same questions from irate customers for the past hour, and fired back at me, "Look, they didn't send us enough of the new stamps. I'm not the person who orders them. It's not my fault. Do you want to speak with the postmaster?"

"Yes I would," I said, only to learn the postmaster was out to lunch and wouldn't return for another half-hour! The situation, from the postal clerk's position, was impossible. He was just as frustrated as I was. Only he didn't care about my situation. He was tired of dealing with irate customers, so he referred me to his boss, who was out to lunch. A real-life example of an impossible situation.

When I finally did speak to the postmaster later that afternoon on the telephone, I learned that there was a run on the new stamp at our post office, but additional stamps would be available the following day. I thanked him for the information and told him about the poor customer service attitude demonstrated by the frustrated postal clerk. The postmaster said he would speak with the person.

I hoped it was a caring confrontation, because the clerk was not to blame for the shortage of postage stamps. He was wrong with his method of dealing with me, a frustrated customer. A little coaching seemed to go a long way with this particular postal clerk. He now smiles more and is much friendlier with all of the customers at our post office. Even if the situation seems impossible, confronting poor performance and coaching inappropriate behavior is necessary.

Don't Overstate Matters

Whenever you overstate a fact or embellish your feelings, you diminish your credibility.

Avoiding these exaggerations permits the employee to preserve his or her self-esteem. Examples:

Don't say: "Your work is totally unacceptable."

Instead say: "Your level of work is not satisfactory."

Don't say: "Your lack of interest cost us a key account."

Instead say: "Your lack of interest is of great concern to me."

Don't say: "You let the whole company down when you didn't respond."

Instead say: "You gave our customers the wrong impression when you did not respond."

When the Agile Manager met Derek Mayfield for breakfast the following week, Derek picked up where he'd left off. "You're not blaming me for the customer canceling that order last week, are you? It wasn't my fault. I called inventory and couldn't get a straight answer from Mary Lou," said Derek. "They are all screwed up in that department."

"Derek, you've done a good job for the two years you've been responsible for the Midwest region," said the Agile Manager. "You accomplished your business plan and exceeded your region's quota last year. You were on target for this year until that order canceled last week."

He continued: "The real problem is that we didn't get the customer the right information when he needed it. Yes, you called Mary Lou in the inventory department to get an answer, but you didn't finish the job. You didn't get an answer and you didn't escalate the situation. With a $400,000 order in jeopardy, you could have called Pete Stancowski or me."

Derek responded immediately, "You know how much I do around here. I work hard for the company. I can't follow up on every request I make. I'm running a region."

"Derek, that's not the issue," said the Agile Manager. "I know how hard you work. I'm not talking about your work ethic. I'm saying your judgment and your actions could have been better. What would you do differently if you had the chance?"

"I should have asked my assistant to follow up with Mary Lou. If he couldn't get an answer from her, I could have called Stancowski to get a straight answer. He's pretty good. But you know he's always in a meeting," said Derek.

"Derek, you know Pete has a voice mail system. You or your assistant could have left him a message," replied the Agile Manager. "If he didn't respond to your message, you could have called me."

"Yes, you're right. I should have left him a message. I guess I wanted to believe Mary Lou would get back to me. I dropped the ball."

"All right," said the Agile Manager. "Here's what I think we can do. It's been just a few days since the customer canceled the order. I've already heard from our VP of engineering. He's willing to come with us to meet with the customer to apologize and to explain how our inventory system and company policy failed, and the changes we've made to see this doesn't happen again. I'm willing to apologize to the customer for our communication failure on the critical information. Can you and Michael set up the appointment for this week?"

"I'd like to be the one to apologize for dropping the ball on communications," said Derek. "It wasn't you, it was me."

The Agile Manager responded, "Derek, can you call Michael right now and ask him to set up the meeting? I think he's got a good relationship with this customer."

"I'll call him on my cell phone right now," said Derek. "Thanks for your help."

"You're welcome, replied the Agile Manager. "I think you and Michael can save this order and this customer. I'm counting on you both."

As Derek dialed Michael Roberts from the breakfast table, the Agile Manager poured another cup of coffee. He knew this was a constructive confrontation. It was also an effective coaching session with Derek Mayfield, a good manager. Derek realized his error, and a poor company policy was changing to become more "customer focused."

The Agile Manager knew that coaching your people each day, and confronting them constructively when necessary, helps them develop their skills. Over time, doing both adds up to significant improvements in productivity. Sipping the fresh cup of coffee, he thought, yes, life is good. Now let's save this order for $400,000 and make it better!

The Agile Manager's Checklist

✔ When confronting an employee, avoid emotion and keep the conversation businesslike.

✔ Schedule the meeting in a neutral spot like a conference room or cafeteria.

✔ Before presenting the problem, spend time building rapport

✔ Present the problem and show why it had an impact on the organization.

✔ Ask for the employee's side of the story.

✔ Discuss solutions jointly.

✔ Follow up and continue to coach.